"*Speedology* ... back to Ameri...

—Emma Goldman

"Astute and keenly observed, Levitch's insights on the human condition call into question our society's self-destructive tendencies. This is an important contribution to a world gone terribly wrong."

—Evel Knievel

"*I have searched **long and hard** for such a book.*"

—Diogenes of Sinope

"**Theatrical shit.**" —Antonin Artaud

"This seditious insanity *sickens* me with a *nauseous* revelation. Why I bothered writing anything (besides *Madness and Civilization*) is beyond me. To think of all the PARTIES I missed!!!"

—Michel Foucault

"**I'd** *date him.*" —Josephine Baker

"*I'd* ***date*** *him.*" —Truman Capote

"*I'd date* ***him.***"

—Speed's First Cousin-Once-Removed

"**Yummy.**" —The Cookie Monster

"He who follows the Cruise knows the Way." —Attila the Hun

"Here is a man who's among the **BEST MINDS OF HIS GENERATION**. He is **AMERICA'S BEST LAST HOPE**. *God help us.*" —Allen Ginsberg

"**READ THIS**. *(I got your back.)*" —Brutus

"Fascinating!" —Claude Lévi-Strauss

"*If only Martha understood me so well.*"
—George Washington

"*OFF with his HEAD!*"
—The Queen of Hearts

"*Rarely has **lasciviousness** figured so prominently in the study of a metropolis, its people, and its history.*"
—Thucydides

"*Sexy?*" —Jay Leno

"In his quest for personal freedom, Speed Levitch has groped toward a sort of **dithering gobbledygook** that's neither revolutionary nor even readable. ***No one will be reading this book in years to come.***"
—Pope John Paul II

"*sexy.*" —Conan O'Brien

"In his quest for personal freedom, Speed Levitch has groped toward the ***most* profound truths** in a way that is as revolutionary as it is entertaining. **People *will be reading this book for years to come.*"**

—Dalai Lama

"**A promising debut.**" —Jesus

"*Speed's a* **voodoo child** *who's* **stoned** *and* **beautiful.** *He knows why* **rock and roll will never die.**"

—Jimi Hendrix

"*A masterpiece!*" —Buddha

"**I recommend this book to managers everywhere.**" —Lee Iacocca

"*I especially love the way Speed Levitch pretends to give a damn about women. Here is a* ***book with no vagina.***"

—Andrea Dworkin

"*I HOPE AMERICA CAN BE MIRACULOUS ENOUGH TO TOLERATE THIS BEAUTIFUL REVOLUTION OF THE MIND EXERCISING ITSELF ON LAUGHTER.*"

—Pee Wee Herman

"After reading this book, I'm convinced we're DOOMED."

—ALAN GREENSPAN

"I *told* you . . ." —NOSTRADAMUS

"Timothy 'Speed' Levitch is a **bad man.**"

—ALEXANDER HAMILTON

"This is *just* great." —SPEED'S MOM

"No matter what **dark wood you inhabit,** ***Speedology: Speed on New York on Speed*** is tourism at its poetic best."

—VIRGIL

"**FUCK THE POLICE!**" —EAZY-E

SPEEDOLOGY

SPEEDOLOGY

Speed on NEW YORK on SPEED

Timothy "SPEED" Levitch

Context Books NEW YORK

2002

Published in the United States of America.
Context Books, New York.

www.contextbooks.com

Designer: Cassandra J. Pappas
Jacket design: Charles Kreloff
*Typefaces: Adobe Minion, Humana Sans ITC, Human Serif ITC,
Human Script ITC, Emigre Matrix, Adobe Bodoni*

Context Books
368 Broadway
Suite 314
New York, NY 10013

Levitch, Timothy, 1970–
Speedology : Speed on New York on speed / Timothy "Speed" Levitch.
p. cm.
isbn 1-893956-29-6 (pbk. : alk. paper)
1. New York (N.Y.)—Description and travel. 2. New York (N.Y.)
—Intellectual life. 3. New York (N.Y.)—Social life and customs.
4. Walking—New York (State)—New York. 5. Levitch, Timothy, 1970—
Homes and haunts—New York (State)—New York. I. Title.
F128.55.L49 2002
974.7'1—dc21 2002010108

ISBN 1-893956-29-6

9 8 7 6 5 4 3 2 1

Manufactured in the United States of America

DEDICATED TO BLACK ROCK CITY

a great metropolis

and its parody

simultaneous

Contents

Speedology

Cruisade

New York City is a great teacher bestowing life lessons upon a mostly slow-learning population. Collecting facts and historical anecdotes about New York City is a hobby for many, but the spiritual knowledge contained by the city is a way of life.

New York City—a great teacher bestowing life lessons on a mostly s l o w -learning population.

The city's traffic, for instance, is spiritual. Congestion is the city-teacher's method of inflicting patience on a population addicted to impatience. A New York City traffic jam is a gathering of international souls brought together to grit their teeth and face one of life's great challenges—sitting still.

As the great tour guide Franz Kafka once wrote, "Impatience is what got us kicked out of Paradise in the first place."

Les Radley, the oldest and most cynical man I've ever known, said to me once, "I hate New York City, but it is my favorite place to get lost." If you take out the words "New York City" and replace them with the word "consciousness," Radley's statement still makes perfect sense.

Tourism springs from the understanding that we are ***all tourists all the time*** and we are touring each other and the tour never ends. We are all landmarks on each other's tour. My favorite landmarks have **heartbeats.**

My New York City is not a statistical, ordered account of place; it is a tantrum. My city is not so easily amused with history, gossip, or a list of places to eat; it is a series of ledges I hang off of.

*

My New York City is not a statistical, ordered account of a place; it is a *tantrum*.

*

The tours in this book are mine, and not necessarily routes to be followed. They are unique karmic predicaments, formed by time and space, meant to incite riots.

They are tours that can be just as successfully performed while sitting in an armchair in a living room in Seattle, walking the streets of the invisible city within.

These are tours to be walked not only by bodies but also by minds. They are pathways to be cartwheeled, danced, and sung as love serenades to possibility.

MESSAGES THE CITY WANTS US TO RECEIVE:

1. THE FASTEST WAY TO ADVENTURE IS TO STAND STILL

All of these walking tours should be done, at least once, standing still.

Boredom is an illusion. Boredom is the continuous state of not noticing that the unexpected is constantly arriving while the anticipated is never showing up. **Boredom is anti-Cruise propaganda. Cruising** is an act, the realization that standing still is exalting.

When we spend ten minutes on a subway platform wondering where the train is, worrying about our destination, obsessed with our need to get to it, we spend ten minutes missing the phenomenal theater unfolding all around us on the subway-platform-cum-stage.

Most people never travel. They simply transport the mad loop of their brain's thoughts from place to place. To truly travel is to stand on fields of yourself where you have never stood before.

The city persecutes anyone who tries to control it. ***Those who enjoy their time in New York City are healthy associates of CHAOS.*** The brain is the organ controlling our need to control the out of control, limiting our limitlessness, and attempting to know the unknowable.

We can beat the brain!

2. THE CITY AS AUTOBIOGRAPHY

We are not visitors, tourists, nor inhabitants of New York City; we *are* New York City. The city is our moving self-portrait and a living art installation carved out of an island of rock, even the cracks in the sidewalk are crying out on the topic of our lives.

The city is a profound opportunity to understand ourselves.

When people say that New York City is expensive they mean it is a challenge. When they say it is busy they mean it is unpredictable. When they say the city is dirty they mean there is too much truth here. What people don't like about New York City is its vitality.

Any appraisal of the outside world is a self-appraisal. This is why a microscopic appreciation of the city is ***a microscopic appreciation of ourselves.***

On the tour, we appreciate beauty out loud, which is us appreciating ourselves and each other out loud.

A tour is happening whenever we are seeking exhilaration together.

The tour guide's journey is a seeking of clarity. The tour guide is so busy figuring out what is happening on the left and what is happening on the right because the tour guide wants to be clear about what the hell is going on. *Clarity is ecstasy in this realm. Ecstasy is the true destination of any tour.*

3. THIS IS NO TIME FOR HISTORICAL ACCURACY

Nothing I say can possibly be defended. I am not interested in being right or wrong; my priority is to be joyous. I do not speak with logic, intellectualization, or fact. ***I speak in explosions.*** I promote thinking and feeling on the topic of ourselves. I promote vacation.

The city does not even know that it has a history, it is far too vital to care about the delusions called the past following us around everywhere. History is an attempt to convince us that the past tense is more significant than the present.

The present tense is a pasta dish and the past tense is oregano, perhaps the marinara sauce, and often the garlic. The past tense flavors this moment of ongoing wow, this current extravaganza surrounding us, this *ENORMOUS NOW!*

Napoleon said history is an agreed upon fiction, and Malcolm McClaren said, history is getting the last word. One man ruled a country, the other man perverted a country. Yet both men were aware that they were taking part in historical events. Even those who learn history are doomed to repeat it if they never reinvent themselves while they're busy learning history.

As a tour guide, I approach history the same way Charlie Parker would approach a jazz standard. I am not here to recapitulate the notes exactly as they were composed but to find myself within the notes and collaborate with what has been before me to chase after everything I could ever be. ***My study of history is mostly an attempt to impress women.***

I use history for one reason and one reason only: to become erotic.

What the story of New York City needs is new mythologies, new sacraments, not the same retelling of a sullen tale told by white men in crisp collars. Let us forego our responsibility to be precise and, instead, let us take on the responsibility of being i n f i n i t e .

4. FEAR IS JOY PARALYZED

The Cruise assumes that fear is here to be overcome because on the other side of every fear is ecstasy. The Cruise assumes that happiness is our purpose in this life.

The anti-Cruise assumes fear is here to be utilized. **Society—the greatest *self-hatred* the Earth has ever witnessed**—is a mediocre improv comedy piece we're all living despite ourselves, one that would be impossible without fear effectively taking on ingenious disguises throughout the adventure of each and every day.

Agenda is utilitarian fear and it quietly controls, utterly, our every day. My friend Plastique once described Manhattan as *Agenda Island.*

WE DO NOT HAVE AGENDAS, AGENDAS HAVE US. Our agendas use our existences, our abilities to exhibit themselves, their goals and their ugliness. These goals are very often more alive than we are.

Pettiness is a triumph of the agenda over life. Pettiness is the one characteristic that can be found in each of Shakespeare's antagonists.

Our fears are tour guides. They are begging to be overcome. On the other side of every fear, ***ecstasy awaits us, hanging out on some romantically lit street corner wondering what's taking us so long.***

5. GREGARIOUSNESS IS GREAT

New York City is a summoning of souls and a tribal ceremony of collected ancient agonies and conflicts brought to a new landscape for healing. A New Yorker is someone who runs wild with healing. A New Yorker is a soul brought to this amazing ceremony to pursue self, and what makes a New Yorker a New Yorker is this pursuit.

As we figure out how to deal with the people in our lives, we are learning how to live. Living is not inherently painful, learning is.

Laughing and crying are both oxygenated learning. ***LAUGHING and CRYING are what happen to learning when it enters our bodies and mixes with our breathing.*** Laughing and crying are what make the city worthwhile.

6. THE SOUL IS THE ONLY LANDMARK

The Empire State Building, the Brooklyn Bridge, and ourselves are all equally extensions of the soul and are all equally manifestations of God's creative consciousness. The tour is not a study of buildings, dates, and statistics. It is a study of ourselves.

The study of anything is a spectator sport until we recognize that our interests are the tour guide to ourselves. Everything we study is a launching pad, an immense and salacious opportunity to learn who we are and who we can be. The "educational system" has trained the average New York tourist to ask "What is the exact height of the Empire State Building?" and "How much did it cost to build?" rather than "WHAT DOES THE EMPIRE STATE BUILDING HAVE TO DO WITH ME?"

I am a cardiovascular exercise meant to make you sweat with the direct experience of appreciating the beauty of us. Beauty is an experience and a vibration, not an intellectualization that leads to cold analysis; beauty is a wet kiss shared between us and our lives.

Salvation** is seeing everything **as it already is.

7. BEING ALIVE IS SEXY

The WORLD is an INVOLUNTARY ORGY. We are all already fantastically naked, exposed, and in love. All the violence of the world is foreplay; orgasms happen when we participate in our lives.

TIME IS our constant SEX PARTNER.

8. WHAT IS CREATED IS DESTROYED

The dance of creation and destruction is the universe's dance and New York City is a fabulous dance floor for many of the universe's vast choreographies. The city is showing us every day that what is created is destroyed. To be a preservationist is to obsess about one side of this equation.

I celebrate the homogenization of Times Square because I

celebrate the high drama of living. **Reality has many flavors and the dead exuberance of repression takes the taste out of it all.**

Many decry the destruction of Pennsylvania Station, the great beaux arts railroad terminal that was knocked down and replaced by the fourth Madison Square Garden. They ask, "If the city is a great teacher, why would it destroy a great building and put a lousy one in its place?" The answer: Pennsylvania Station was too beautiful. The anecdote may be a catastrophe from a preservationist's point of view, but it is a masterpiece from a dramatist's.

It's just the way Tennessee Williams would have written it.

Many will then ask, "Why is the city issuing forth these dramas?" The answer: *the **city** wants to **entertain us.***

The city is trying to entertain us with our own lives, a great dramatist constantly turning our lives upside down and desecrating whatever has just been declared holy. New York City is openly assaulting all addictions to closure, all stubbornness, and all ego.

As is the goal of any great dramatist, *the city is interested in **inflicting** COMPASSION upon the population and melting its masks.*

The city goes on every day no matter who or what gets destroyed within its boundaries. So do we. It does not matter what happens in our dramas. We do not end, we are just like the city that persists and thrives in a state of continuous destruction and decay, rebirth and growth.

The city's very existence is proof that we are much more afraid of immortality than death.

9. THE MOST SIGNIFICANT THING ABOUT SUFFERING IS THAT WE'RE ALL DOING IT

Alienation is ourselves forgetting how good we are at energizing each other and the fact that we all suffer is proof that we are all in this together.

The interconnectedness of the human race is real and we are communicating with each other in ways we are not even aware of. The city is a contest of our joys and joylessnesses. Joy spreads like wildfire, and in the contest between them, joy is the force that is actually self-sufficient, whereas joylessness is the truly parasitic partner. This means that **the ENTIRE CITY could be ENTIRELY JOYOUS if our COURAGE would stand up for us.**

Suffering is hesitant celebration.

The only reason people do not look each other in the eye during rush hour is because deep down they know they are all lovers and eye contact is the spark that could instantaneously lift them into episodes of orgiastic lovemaking and they would miss the evening news.

10. OUR TRUE SELVES ARE THE GREATEST PARTIES EVER THROWN

You are a better PARTY than you have ever been to.

To listen carefully to New York City is to be listening carefully to the greatest partier, the most original and flamboyant figure any of us will ever know.

Therefore, to listen carefully to New York City is to be original.

Walt Whitman said, "Some are lost in nature and must come to the city to find themselves."

The young people who move to New York City and fall in

love with it are, most of all, falling in love with their new place in the world.

To live in a city is to realize that **life is a procession of different versions of ourselves that we meet over time.** Evolving is the meeting between who you were and who you just became. A city's greatness rests in the intensity of its transformations, and in the transformations it stirs within us.

Finally, a city's greatness depends on the quality of its voyeurism and exhibitionism.

11. HAVING FAITH IN HUMANITY IS SUPPOSED TO BE FUN

FUN IS active FAITH. Faith IS the CELEBRATION of "I DON'T KNOW."

The city is a bravely unfolding movie entertaining us so effectively we are hypnotized by it. The movie is a comedy about mammals in a movie taking the movie seriously and deciding it is a tragedy.

These tours are **recommendations on how to dress for the unknown.** Tips on how to seduce the self. Each of New York City's neighborhoods are attempts to create the right lighting for us to get comfortable together on the dance floor. Each neighborhood has the possibility of becoming a party where everyone is truly out for everyone else's happiness, where loneliness is clearly an illusion and togetherness is inescapable, a party where the wise are recognized for being those who are funny and fun simultaneously, where the frivolous and the courageous recognize they have a lot in common, and our lust and our compassion finally exchange phone numbers.

People often ask me if I think New York City is a great city. "No," I reply, "it's still **a party ON THE VERGE of being fun.**"

12. I AM NOT GETTING LAID

I want to make it clear, from the beginning, that I am not currently getting laid as I write this and this fact colors everything I say. It's the one statement that makes perfect sense of Nietzsche's work.

This book was written during a period of enforced celibacy, enforced upon me by the city for the city's own reasons.

In any case, it should be known by the reader . . . I have tremendous sexual problems.

In the middle of some of these tours, Natasha-at-Times-Simone enters. When she appears the reader can be assured that the tour has collided with my need for a woman, and therefore, ***the tour has officially become an outcry for love and an opulent TANTRUM.***

I met Natasha when she was a lap dancer giving me a lap dance under her stripper pseudonym, Simone. Neither women shared their body with me because they are not my lovers; they are my symbionts.

New York real estate has thrust me into their embrace. When you are a couch surfer desperately hanging off the ledge of this city, salvation is a woman with an apartment who cannot stand to be alone.

Recently this anthill woke up to the fact that being stepped on *is* a possibility. It was at this time that Natasha-at-Times-Simone became Simone-Flopping-Before-Audiences-of-Natasha and the young, grande-dame enchantress of this distressed metropolis became a living personification of her city's feelings.

Natasha-Disdaining-Simone, I am just a man who sleeps on your floor, and it is from this angle that I have seen episodes of New York's history alive in you.

Simone-Dizzy-in-the-Presence-of-Natasha, live! You are a *New Yorker*—a piece of a vast living spontaneity sprawled across a series of islands. Together let's find our way into the freshest, newest, most innovative way to fall in love.

Keep It Alive!

—Timothy "Speed" Levitch

TO REORDER YOUR UPS DIRECT THERMAL LABELS:

1. Access our supply ordering web site at ups.com or Contact UPS at 800-877-8652.
2. Please refer to Label #02774006 when ordering.

WF

Label #02774006

TotalCampus.com Packing Slip
1214 Commerce Ct. #300
Lafayette, CO 80026

SKU	Product Name	Qty	Unit Price
1893956296N	Speed's New York	1	$11.47

For Customer Service Questions: http:\\www.TotalCampus.com\store\customerservice.asp

Thank You For Ordering from TotalCampus.com

Broadway the Renegade

In the city there's a thousand things I wanna say to you!
—The Jam

WE BEGIN AT 10TH STREET AND BROADWAY:

The city is a great and brave individual spreading the message of individuality. Broadway is the path that follows its own path. This is the one street that refuses to conform to the **GRID PLAN**—the system of streets organized by our agendas rather than our hearts. A PARENTAL DISCRETION INFLICTED ON A GROWING CHILD-CITY; real estate speculators doing to the city what their parents had done to them. If New York City is great, it is because it continues to attract young people who resist lethargy and refuse to follow the paths of others. **There is a Broadway running through all of us.**

Broadway wants us to get back in touch with our stirring, to feel *stirred* again.

La Rochefoucauld wrote, "Many would never fall in love if they had not heard of it."

I am a tour guide because I am here to root on Broadway and participate in its mission. Due to this, I am now in photo albums all over the world.

The brave, unique, painterly stroke that *is* Broadway charges across the entire length of Manhattan Island and is a part of more neighborhoods than any other street.

Broadway is the **Albany Post Road.** This path was discovered by Native Americans who were listening closely to the vibrations of the Earth. **Broadway is millennia of footprints upon footprints.**

Broadway becomes **Route 9** north of Manhattan. It channels through the **Bronx** and then into **Westchester County.** There, Broadway is rolling hills and fields, as it eventually rides into the **Adirondack Mountains**, becoming monumental, swelling earth.

Broadway begins with the oldest park in Manhattan, called **Bowling Green Park.** The genesis is a widening delta of concrete with a center of green turf imbued with the history of revolution. In 1776, the statue of King George the Third stood where the fountain flows today. It was beheaded after the first public reading of the Declaration of Independence. An artist's rendering of this event was a bestselling lithograph in Paris, eerily foreshadowing the regicide that would happen there in 1791. (**For more about Bowling Green Park, refer to "Wall Street: the Story of What Happened to Our Intimacy;" for more about revolution, refer to yourselves.**)

Where Manhattan Island ends, Broadway becomes a bridge called the **Broadway Bridge.** The bridge that Broadway becomes bestrides the channel where the Hudson and Harlem Rivers conjoin for a brief lapse of psychotic tides that the Dutch called **Spuyten Duyvil.** The confluence of these rivers is a whirlwind of Mother Nature's power, a moat and a hazard that has sunk many ships and drowned many souls.

This intersection of **10th Street and Broadway** *is one of New York City's great orations on the topic of happenstance.* The curvature of Broadway that happens here was created by several forces. Many of these forces are incomprehensible and beyond names. One of the identifiable forces was a man named **Henry Brevoort.**

At 10th Street and Broadway, at the turn of the eighteenth century, Henry Brevoort owned an **apple orchard.** As Broadway was being paved over, the new northbound boulevard was about to encroach upon several trees of knowledge. Brevoort insisted that the road divert itself to the west so as to skirt the corner of his apple orchard. The only echo of Brevoort's dramatic dance in and around the ramparts and springlike effervescences of the Garden of Eden is the curve in Broadway it left behind.

In New York, we parade our glories and our persecutions up and down a boulevard that is curved because it supported a man and his own deluded vision of Eden. ***THE ESSENCE OF ALL ORIGINAL THOUGHT IS A PERSONAL, VAULTED VISION OF PARADISE.***

There was a time when this city considered the fruit of knowledge more significant than the straightness of a road! **(For more on this see, "Central Park: Mother Nature Is Cosmopolitan.")**

Jazz musicians in the Depression era referred to New York City as the **"Big Apple"** on their concert tour itineraries that were filled with cities they called apples. All the cities they visited and serenaded provided for them life, knowledge, and juiciness, but New York City was ***the juiciest, most incredible fiasco.***

***The Big Apple* is where we are *overwhelmed* with this gift of being alive, living out visions of being *overwhelmed*.**

Cosmopolitans are tortured by our collective exile from Paradise, and we are all extravagant defenders of Eve. City dwellers believe that Eve was right, but her timing was off.

Broadway proves to us that the city is an enormous benevolence underlying every originality happening within it.

Being in New York City is a SWIFT KICK to the consciousness. To be *on Broadway* is to be living out this truth. This is an original place and when we listen to it, we are original.

In the **Museum of Modern Art's permanent collection (at 53rd Street between Fifth and Sixth Avenues) Piet Mondrian's** painting entitled *Broadway Boogie Woogie* is the first **neoplastic painting** of his fifty-year neoplastic career in which he did not use the color black. Mondrian's Neoplasticism is an attempt to build an art form that is truly a departure from this world and its references. He moved to New York City at the age of seventy-one. He set up a studio on 57th Street. While painting *Broadway Boogie Woogie*, Mondrian recorded in his journal his sudden disagreements with virtually his entire body of work. He accused himself of using black lines to express in his paintings what fields of color are meant to express; this, he concluded, is the difference between drawings and paintings.

This was a seventy-one-year-old man experiencing a revolution. Perhaps it was incited by his dialogue with the city's grid plan. MAYBE THE STREETS EXPLAINED TO HIM THAT THEIR PERPENDICULAR ALIGNMENT BORED THEM. They were so exciting because of the random choreography of human activity happening all over them.

There is nothing in my life that is on a right angle.

From any corner of 10th and Broadway, the straight line of Broadway's southern vein is appalling. It is clear that we are standing at a point of crisis in Broadway's journey. When Broadway enters this intersection, it is a linear primrose path to Paradise heading in a straight line. By the time it leaves this intersection, **Broadway is a mad trajectory twisting to the left,** suddenly heading northwest *for reasons only it can* **truly understand.**

The NYU dormitory **Brittany Hall**, once a hotel, on the northwest corner of 10th and Broadway, has an art gallery embedded in it that is flashing the sidewalk. It is called **Windows on Broadway.** An art gallery is a landmark of transformation and it seems fitting to have an ongoing, changing visual display happening on this intersection where Broadway experiences such a rite of passage.

The grid plan's first incarnation is as a blueprint—a theory drawn across a page. The grid plan was designed by real estate speculators who were attempting to catalyze real estate speculation. These real estate speculators were once children whose evolution became synonymous with their parents', and so the city's evolution is only allowed to occur according to the dictates of the real estate speculator's personal psychological limitations and selfish motivations.

We all have a blueprint that we must DEFY. Much of our lives are spent standing with our parents, examining the original blueprint that they had drawn up before we were born. This is the blueprint that maps out who we're supposed to be and what our lives are supposed to say. When parents get upset about life decisions their children are making, it is because the child is not acting in accordance with the original blueprint.

The blueprint is the parent's design made for the sake of the parent's emotional stability and so-called sanity. It is the design for the child they want, for the child who will finally convince them that their lives have meaning. When the child makes decisions in accordance with the parental blueprint, the child's life has become more a dissertation on the parents' life than an actual life being lived.

Every time BROADWAY CROSSES the GRID, BIG THINGS happen.

Natasha-Evolving-Despite-Simone once mentioned to me, "Broad and way—the conjunction of the two is a huge opening." I couldn't agree more.

Above us, the illuminated steeple here at 10th and Broadway is **Grace Church.** Designed by **James Renwick** in 1846, Grace Church is visible. Its loftiness, its objectivity and its quietude exudes a floating confidence that illuminates each nocturne with transcendence.

Across the street, the low-lying commercial building stripped of its adornments, seated on the southwest corner of **11th and Broadway** is the **Hotel St. Denis.** This was a major hotel of New York City's mid-nineteenth-century era. It housed **Abraham Lincoln** several times, **"Buffalo" Bill Cody, P. T. Barnum,** and **Ulysses S. Grant.**

At the back of the St. Denis lobby, ***note the black wrought-iron staircase that still believes it is ascending for the benefit of great men, carrying the weight of their big thoughts.***

On May 11, 1877, **Alexander Graham Bell** sent awe through a private audience of prominent guests on the second-floor parlor room of the Hotel St. Denis as he demonstrated his brand-new invention—the telephone.

Technology is an extension of human potential. Computers, radios, televisions, and telephones are all materializations of our will to be interconnected. **(For more on interconnectedness, see "The Midtown Rush Hour Tour.")**

Bell was one of many shaman-citizens innovating the world along the banks of Broadway, a raging river at the turn of the century cascading into Midtown and the twentieth century.

At **Fifth Avenue,** Broadway's self-realization creates a sharp triangle where one of the most photogenic, eccentric structures of architectural history has risen, the **Flatiron Building.** A wind tunnel was created by the Flatiron's flat façade and Fifth Avenue, to this day inciting the winds famous for lifting women's skirts into the air. In 1903, in the height of Victorian New York, Broadway was mocking Victorianism with an effortlessness and grace that Harpo Marx somewhere was inspired by. **(For more about the lewdness of 23rd Street and Fifth Avenue, refer to "We Do Not Fear Death As Much As We Fear Immortality: Madison Square Park")**

When **Broadway** boldly crosses **Seventh Avenue**, it does so in the name of following its own destiny! The crossing creates **Times Square.**

Times Square was pasture right up until 1905–06. It is a twentieth-century dream actualized.

TIMES SQUARE HAS RECENTLY BEEN DRESSED UP TO MAKE PEOPLE WHO DO NOT QUESTION THINGS MORE COMFORTABLE.

To those who criticize Times Square's current incarnation: If you want to save the world, save yourself first. If you want to make Times Square a better place, be a better person. It is merely you.

Times Square is not a typical city square à la San Marco Square in Venice or Red Square in Moscow. In fact, it is not even a square.

Times Square cannot *be contained* in a SQUARE. It is **too busy** being ***inundated*** by its *own* **COMMOTION.** How many times have I stood on Times Square with visitors to the city as they turned and asked me, "Where is Times Square?"

Geometry is a complicated joke told by a brave Dionysian whose punch line is an ongoing rational descent/ascent into irrationality. Axioms are meta-ironic opportunities for instrumentation. This is all because **Euclid was an alcoholic and Pythagoras could not be trusted alone with his body**, and therefore, reflexively his body could not be trusted left alone with himself.

Where Broadway crosses over **66th Street**, one of the very rare vista views in the city has become the stage for **Lincoln Center.** Lincoln Center, designed by **Philip Johnson,** is a suave acropolis and a status quo performing arts center. Broadway has always been the theater district of the city, and it was the original **Great White Way** because after electricity got mixed up with Edison it was always electrified. **(For more about the Great White Way, refer to "We Do Not Fear Death As Much As We Fear Immortality: Madison Square Park," or refer to your divine spark.)**

Where Broadway crosses over **Convent Avenue** and **168th Street** is hallowed ground. **Malcolm X** was killed there.

When Broadway moves through **Washington Heights**, bear in mind that this is where George Washington lost New York to the British.

With every twist and turn, Broadway declares childhood, a reawakening, and issues forth great feasts for curiosity.

This is true for all the rebellions we make, for all the revolutionary turns we take from our grid plans.

* * *

BROADWAY is here for us to walk on and REBEL with!

Wall Street: The Story of What Happened to Our Intimacy

Did you ever feel like you've been cheated?!
—Johnny Rotten

I look forward to the day when our lives won't be printed on dollar bills!
—Clifford Odets

The mythological gesture that gave birth to this land was not as mystical as a lady of the lakes emanating from the waters with Excalibur, or as romantic as a dare between two brothers and seven hills. The mythological gesture that gave birth to this land was a **transaction.**

A **transaction** is the most mediocre form of human intercourse. It is an exchange of mutual fictions rather than of true feeling. It is a way for two people to take at the same time, together. *There is more human sharing in murder than there is in a* ***transaction.***

THE TRANSACTION—THE MOST MEDIOCRE FORM OF HUMAN INTERCOURSE.

A transaction is bad sex happening all over the city, all day, everywhere. The gesture emanates simultaneously from our fear and our need for each other. While handing someone a dollar bill, we are necessarily entering his personal space but keeping ourselves at arm's distance.

There is so much uninspired *sex in the city* it keeps me up at night. Just as Natasha-Ignoring-Simone does.

We all need a hug and we even want to get close to each other, but we are afraid of each other. The transaction develops from this contradiction. Anyone is invited into our immediate periphery as long as they have a constructive, profitable reason to be there.

Therefore, to be profitable is to be good at *not* giving.

The *transaction* is the gesture at the beginning of the mythological tale called "New York City." **Peter Minuit,** a German representing Dutch interests, purchases the island from a passing Native American tribe in 1624. The deal was a fiction. The Native Americans accepting the barter were just visitors themselves. What was actually transacted were chickens and dry goods and red wheelbarrows. The Native Americans probably walked away from the encounter talking about the strange, generous man who had just been washed ashore and given them all these great things.

The original sexual intercourse that gives birth to the idea of Nieuw Amsterdam is uninspired sex between men who did not speak the same language, linguistically or spiritually. New York City, likewise, was created to be a great escape from sharing.

Wall Street was a wall built officially by the original European settlers of this island to protect themselves from the English who were to the north in Massachusetts. Subliminally, the wall was built to protect them from the boundless possibilities of an unlabeled continent laid out before them.

IN THE FACE OF BOUNDLESSNESS, HUMAN BEINGS HAVE A TENDENCY TO BUILD WALLS.

Wall Street is still a wall. The wooden barricade of the seventeenth century was torn down long ago and used by the British for firewood, but the consciousness that gives Wall Street meaning is a colossal fortress built between ourselves and our hearts.

MONEY IS OUR ONGOING ATTEMPT TO REPLACE ***intimacy***, and therefore, money is our painful lesson plan teaching us that there is no replacement for intimacy.

Welcome to Wall Street!

WE BEGIN AT PETER MINUIT PLAZA IN FRONT OF THE STATEN ISLAND FERRY TERMINAL:

Behind us, stretching along the water, is the **Staten Island Ferry Terminal**, green with oxidation. During the 1890s, there were more than one hundred ferry boats launching in a hundred different directions from Manhattan Island. The Staten Island Ferry, the most famous of the few still sailing, is a twenty-five minute, free oceanic journey. It is a far faster and easier-going way to view the **Statue of Liberty** than the "Liberty Ferry" that sails directly to the statue. (**See "A Tour of the Statue of Liberty: Stay Free**).

On an evening tour, I stood with a Dutch woman on the Staten Island Ferry as we sailed toward Manhattan. The sky and the city together formed a living El Greco painting, and the view from the boat seemed unlikely, and as we got closer to the shore, it seemed impossible. The Dutch lady asked me, "Why all the lights? Why don't they turn off the lights if no one is in the buildings?" I replied, "Because ***New York City is a movie star.*** It's posing."

The rational Dutch lady looked at me, confused. I cackled. Together, we were a complete manifestation of all the primary ingredients that gave birth to this phantasm before us.

Through the trees, across **Battery Park**, one can still stare out to the succulent spot, in the middle of the watery New York Harbor, where the great cruiser **Verrazano** stood sometime in 1524, as he put it, "at the mouth of a great river, between two hills."

This incredible harbor with its direct, flowing entrance into the **Atlantic Ocean** is what initially brought the polite marauders we call "Europeans" to this place. The island itself was a giant rock and a ridiculous place to live. Here we are standing on landfill. ***This patch of land is not historically accurate*** from the point of view of the glaciers who, in their last melting breath, sculpted this island in a passionate attempt to leave their imprint on the world.

The radically curved skyscraper in front of us, **17 State Street**, echoes the original shoreline of the island when it was purely a remnant left behind by the **Ice Age.**

If you ever get really depressed and feel surrounded by seemingly unsolvable problems, remember that we are all living between two ice ages. This thought has saved my life on a couple of occasions.

The **Seton House** is the Georgian house sitting next to 17 State Street. It is the only survivor of a row of Georgian mansions that skirted this original edge of the city, overlooking the harbor. This house was spared because it was the residence of the first American-born saint, **Elizabeth Ann Seton.**

The Staten Island Ferry boat was invented by a dynamic flesh experiment in survivalism

called Cornelius Vanderbilt. The Vanderbilt family was an upper-middle-class family living on Staten Island at the beginning of the nineteenth century. According to legend, the fifteen-year-old Cornelius asked his mother for a hundred-dollar loan to buy a few wooden rafts for the purpose of transporting his friends and relatives between Staten Island and Manhattan. He returned to her a month later with a thousand dollars in profit.

By the time Vanderbilt is eighteen, he has a fleet of schooners that are fast enough to outrun the British ships during their siege of New York in 1812, making him the major food and provisions provider for the entire city during that time. He also uses the ships' dexterity to encroach upon the highly profitable trade of mussels and clams in Maryland, Virginia, and New York. At the age of twenty-five, having already invented three different fortunes, Vanderbilt focuses his concentration on railroads. His **New York Central Railroad Company** becomes the rail company that turns the entire eastern seaboard of the United States into a cute, primrose path to paradise. **Paradise is 42nd Street and Park Avenue.** Inadvertently, Cornelius Vanderbilt gives birth to Midtown Manhattan by making the small depot on 42nd Street his railroad's hub. (**See "The Midtown Rush Hour Tour."**)

The most important fact about Cornelius Vanderbilt is that he was a bad father. He was one of the wealthiest self-made men in the world, and yet he still felt the need to compete with his children. He believed he could absolve his sins of violence against life with cold, hard cash. His fortune was a surrogate for all the human relationships he missed out on. His incredible resume is actually a list of excuses as to why he never had time to sit in his living room. His empire and his board meetings: all of it was an elaborate escape from intimacy.

Cornelius Vanderbilt—not a good father.

Capitalism, a giant crib, does not reward those who pursue the fullest amplifications of self, it rewards those who have given up that pursuit to meekly settle down with visions of themselves as mediocre children taught to dream. Fathers can disown sons if the sons turn out to be bad investments. Love is having everyone's goals in alignment. **(Refer to *Death of a Salesman* by Arthur Miller.)**

The entire idea of an economy was developed by those using money for identity. An economy is a society's method of containing its people in every facet of their lives except for sex and faith. It is **THE ONGOING STRATEGY HATCHED BY THE OLDER GENERATION to subjugate the younger generation.** Economy exists for the sole purpose of keeping us from staring into each other's eyes.

A capitalistic economy, a libertarian economy, a Keynesian economy, an economy of the invisible hand, and a communist economy all insist, without ever stating it, that our contributions to them are more important than our contributions to each other.

We are standing at the base of **Water Street**, so called because this area where we stand was originally water. As we float down **Water Street**, the **Brooklyn Bridge** is off to our right, starboard. **John Augustus Roebling**, the visionary and architect of this bridge, went insane when he saw it actualized. His story, mythological, is the same as Doctor Frankenstein's. His creation thrilled him in dreams and terrified him in oxygen.

Completed in 1884, many men died during the construction of this bridge and felt justified dying in its name. This is because the bridge, much more than a bridge in their eyes, is the symbolic consummation of manifest destiny—the American usurpation of the North American continent. Therefore, **the bridge can also be called a GRAVESTONE.**

I highly recommend walking across the Brooklyn Bridge.

The bridge is very collapsible in the imagination, and even more so when actually underneath your feet. In the early days of the bridge's career, many people were trampled to death while crossing it. **Large pedestrian crowds would feel the vibrations undulating in the bridge's suspension and would unanimously panic.** Assuming the bridge was collapsing, the crowds would run off in disorganized hordes, trampling each other to death.

No one dared observe that the crowd's reaction to its deadly feelings of imbalance were, from the bridge's point of view, a contribution to its ongoing perfect balance. This dance between balance and imbalance is a part of every rush hour, but these were the truest rush hours New York City has ever known.

Once, I had a couch-surfing sleepover on the large manly couch of **Norman Mailer** in his amazing pad in Brooklyn Heights. (The invitation came from Mailer's son, **Steven**, a lovely man and a marvelous actor. Norman never knew I was there.) The raised ceiling of the apartment had tall walls cascading with hammocks and platforms, rope and ladders. I had never been in an apartment that felt so much like a tall ship. From each platform of the place, a new view of the Brooklyn Bridge and the harbor awaited.

Tossing and turning in the thick linen while my head rested on a toughened, manly pillow, I noticed a large hardcover book—the fourtieth anniversary issue of *Playboy*, a limited edition that contained a celebratory abridged photographic history of all the playmates who had ever posed nude for the magazine. On the inside of the cover, **Hugh Hefner** had written in large magic-marker hieroglyphics, "Norm—It's been a great forty years . . . Love, Hef."

I stared at the photographs of nude women from my favorite decade of centerfolds—the 1950s—and I realized another truthful life lesson while staring between a certain woman's thighs from 1955. There is more history of New York City in a

Playboy centerfold than in the entire *Encyclopedia of New York* or any other academic study of the place. The *Playboy* centerfold is an autobiography of our heartbeats and our genitals. *The Encyclopedia of New York* is written by our brains to build a better tomorrow for our self-doubt. In my analogy, I didn't mean to exclude womankind or their own rebellions against alphabetizing, but you can understand, I was on Norman Mailer's couch.

We coast farther up Water Street until we see **Broad Street** experiencing its genesis on our left. Take a left onto Broad Street. Broad Street was the original canal flowing from the East River through the Nieuw Amsterdam trading post. This is why Broad Street is much wider than the other more claustrophobic streets of Nieuw Amsterdam around us.

In mythology, water represents the unconscious. Mythology's view of Broad Street, therefore, would be as an elongated unconsciousness paved over. Broad Street is, in mythological terms, repression. Feel the repression under your feet. *Tread carefully along the sidewalk and see if you can feel* ***the repressed unconsciousness of this place thumping from below,*** *then take note of the yellow building on our right.* This is **Fraunces Tavern.**

Fraunces Tavern was the James Delancey house, and it became Fraunces's tavern in 1757. Fraunces eventually became George Washington's personal chief steward. The original Continental Congress was founded inside the tavern, and George Washington said his farewell to the officers in his army here. This is a reconstruction of the original structure which burned many times in several different fires throughout the nineteenth century. The reconstruction was executed by "The Sons of the Revolution of New York State" and their agenda.

Today, **FRAUNCES TAVERN** is a museum and a restaurant.

When one peruses the modern incarnation of Fraunces Tavern, one realizes that reconstruction has an aftertaste that is similar to mouthwash. It is a clean, polite study of carnage and despair that results in pristine nostalgia and vague philanthropy. Most attempts to re-create history fail to understand that history is not a documentation as much as it is a sensation. When I visited the Holocaust Museum in Washington, D.C., I felt totally safe and secure, and I passed through without one insult, without one threat made on my life. **WHEN I VISIT ELLIS ISLAND TODAY, I FEEL THE AIR-CONDITIONING MUCH MORE THAN THE POSSIBILITY OF BEING DENIED ENTRY TO THE UNITED STATES BECAUSE I HAVE GOUT.**

Go inside to the new bar in Fraunces Tavern, get a round of drinks, and toast to the fact that all reconstruction is taxidermy. Toast to this place, another attempt historians have made to exclude, and therefore absolve, themselves from history. History is not something to be documented. It is something to be felt. How does it feel to me? *History is fifteen thousand years of neurotic disequilibrium breathing on the back of my neck.*

Walk steadily up Broad Street. Note the narrow streets all around you. Claustrophobic in feeling, many of these Lower Manhattan streets will never see sunlight again. These are the oldest streets of Manhattan Island. These streets were designed by the Dutch of the early seventeenth century. Welcome to Nieuw Amsterdam.

As we cross **Pearl Street**, feel the presence of New York City's first **printing press**, the mascot of modern European civilization, which sat at **81 Pearl Street.** As we cross over **South William Street**, listen for the Hebraic and Ladino prayers still floating in the wind as they emanate from New York City's first synagogue, which stood at **26 South William Street.** The synagogue was built in 1730 and was engulfed, along with six hundred other buildings in this area, by the great fire of 1835.

The fire of 1835 happened in mid-December during freezing

temperatures and a blowing gale. The water from the firemen's hoses froze before even reaching the fire. One of the major fires of early American history, it wiped out most of the original Nieuw Amsterdam architecture and led to the utilization of cast iron and other new materials by builders of the city anxious to build inflammable buildings. (**For more on this, refer to "A Tour of SoHo, or How to Render Sexual Frustation Obsolete."**)

As we cross over **Beaver Street**, taste some of the great food of past generations served in **Delmonico's**, the original premier restaurant of New York founded in 1827. It was also the site of some of New York's original premier gossip.

As we move farther north, let us take a moment to view the tiny street called **Exchange Place**, not as a street but as an art installation. In the context of this neighborhood, the name of this street is a reference to money trading. Viewed as an enormous, autonomous sculpture, Exchange Place is a series of sexual longings exchanged but not shared between a vast variety of shafts and concave angles. There are complicated sexual postures formed between these gigantic shapes, but no consummation. The skyscrapers attain their altitude due to wanton lust. The human beings moving around this living sculpture that takes up an entire city block do their own version of exchanging instead of sharing, thus echoing the vast shapes that dwarf them. This sculpture is here as a reminder that **THE MAIN THING THAT COMES FROM REPLACING *intimacy* WITH MONEY IS THAT NO ONE *gets laid*.**

The neoclassical edifice facing Exchange Place and sitting on a slight curvature of the street line is the **New York Stock Exchange.**

This is the landmark of pulling in and out of stocks. This is the world where an ideal day is a day spent buying low and selling high. This is a place where nonparticipatory attitudes and general hesitations about living life are actively convincing themselves that they have a purpose. This is the embodiment of **cynicism.**

CYNICISM is a nonparticipatory LETHARGY aimed at our afternoons. Just like a good stockbroker knows how to pull out in time for downward slopes in a stock, a good cynic knows how to pull out of an afternoon, meekly running from circumstances not going his or her way. Cynicism is the effective use of noncommunication with the world, which leads to the effective use of noncommunication with our fellow human beings, which is capitalism.

Anti-**Cruise** views an **afternoon** as something to be utilized and/or contained in the name of **self-preservation** and **self-promotion.** The anti-Cruise only participates in an afternoon if there is practical necessity, or if the events and emotions involved are very favorable. The anti-Cruise attends a party only for the political reasons of making an appearance, never to actually party.

The CRUISE is here to completely EMBRACE the world. The Cruise views any afternoon as a masterpiece of art and a daily opportunity to fall in love with the world. The Cruise is here to participate in every afternoon regardless of the results: ascension or demolition.

The Stock Exchange is open to the public on weekdays for free tours during business hours. There is a small museum exhibition one passes through before reaching the soundproof booth that hangs over the main room. The abridged history of the exchange inadvertently proves for all time that MATERIALISM IS THE UTILIZATION of the FEAR OF OTHER PEOPLE'S OPINIONS.

Once inside the soundproof booth, one looks down upon a giant playpen filled with children dressed up in different costumes playing a game that involves frantic gesturing, screaming, and jumping up and down. Even though the booth is soundproof, one can still hear the children's collective air of self-importance. The Stock Exchange and all who monitor it are addicted to their own suspense. "A bear market" and "a bull market": two opposites thriving off of each other. The whole operation would crumble and become a forgotten ruin if it did not mirror a casino. If it were only a place to make money or exclusively a place to lose money, there would be no drama.

In front of the Stock Exchange, is the **buttonwood tree.** It was under this tree, in 1792, that the first meeting of brokers took place, and today, this buttonwood tree still stands in front of the Stock Exchange, ceremoniously facing Wall Street.

WHEN COMMERCE ENTERED THIS THIN STREET IN FRONT OF US CALLED "WALL STREET," ALL THE CURRENCIES OF THE WORLD DISCOVERED THE SAME GOD.

Take a moment with this sad, sickly sapling reaching out for sunlight through the wrought-iron cage in which it is incarcerated. A steel grate lies over its root system. There are usually miscellaneous scraps of garbage piled around the tree's base. It is less a tree than it is a symbol. ***The tree is a piece of nature, shot and stuffed and hung over a god's fireplace.***

It is clear where this intersection's priorities lie when one compares the size of the Stock Exchange's façade to nature's representative here. With this vision, the city is exhibiting how much more seriously we take our illusions than we do our reality.

*

The Buttonwood Tree in front of the Stock Exchange—less a *tree*, more a *symbolic gesture*.

*

Perception is a dogmatic gesture. For instance, I can point to the statue across the street from the Stock Exchange, kitty-corner from the buttonwood tree, and tell you that it is a portrayal of **George Washington** taking the oath of office as the first president of the United States. This statue will now take on a significance and a symbolism for you that is, perhaps, unstoppable.

Now take a deep breath and close your eyes for a solid moment of centrality that emanates from within. When we reopen our eyes and view this statue again, let us try to view it with complete objectivity, bereft of any specific ideological accoutrement or national pride. Open your eyes. What do you see? There is a large man in eighteenth-century garb with an expression of need on his face. He is not smiling. He has one hand resting on air, the palm facing the Earth. His other hand is being held out and this hand being held out is half clenched.

George Washington is hoping someone will hold his hand. He is standing here, in bronze, among throngs of people, waiting for someone to reach out and hold his hand.

Let us close our eyes and breathe again, reopen them, and this time view the statue as George Washington, the first president of the United States, waiting for someone to hold his hand. This statue is the most profound encapsulation of American history I have ever seen.

The statue is an example of history being felt by someone more than history being documented. It was sculpted by **John Quincy Ward** and by the vibrations of early American history—that incredible drama, dancing around this corner right now.

The building behind George Washington is the **Federal Hall National Memorial**, built in 1842 as the U.S. Custom House to replace the second City Hall. It was in that building that **Peter**

Zenger, an early-eighteenth-century journalist, was tried for sedition after printing mockeries in a local publication about an English government official. Zenger's acquittal plants the seeds of a "free press" in the collective unconscious. THE RIGHT TO exhibit our opinions IS ONLY RESTRICTED NOW BY OUR OWN self-censorship.

Here, at the corner of Wall Street and Broad, in 1765, the **Stamp Act Congress** met and drafted a declaration of rights and a list of grievances. This was the first formal congregation of American colonists to stand together in a room and use the phrase "Taxation without representation." These were the words that would spark the war with England.

Here, at the corner of Wall Street and Broad, on July 18, 1776, the **Declaration of Independence** was read aloud. The Declaration has become one of history's great guidelines on how to theorize a miracle. America is an endeavor trying not only to declare itself but also to experience itself. American tourists prefer to ride sightseeing buses through New York because **THERE IS TOO MUCH AMERICA HERE** and it is easier to deal with if it is all a blur.

New York City was occupied by the British for seven out of the eight years of the American Revolutionary War, and the building that stood on this corner was their headquarters throughout the entire occupation. After the war, the **Northwest Ordinance** was passed by the **Second Continental Congress** from this corner. This was the Americans' first attempt to create a country with a centralized government. The democracy they eventually craft on this corner has now outlived even the Athenian democracy.

Pierre L'Enfant, the designer of Washington, D.C., and Indianapolis, Indiana, renovated the second City Hall building in 1789. When he finished the remodeling, the building that once stood on this corner became the capitol of the United States. Here, on the corner of Wall Street and Broad, the same Congress that now meets in Washington, D.C., met for the first time on March 4, 1789. As their first official act, Congress counted the electoral ballots for the first presidential election and noted the unanimous vote for George Washington as the president of the brand-new country.

On Wall Street and Broad, on April 30, 1789, shortly before the fall of the Bastille in Paris, George Washington took his oath of office. He has been standing here ever since waiting for someone to hold his hand.

When I worked on the double-decker tour bus, my vehicular lover and the erogenous center of my postadolescent life, we used to turn on this corner every single tour. Three or four or five times a day, I would point to this George Washington monument and feel the entire bus sway to the left as *passengers from all over the world LEANED OVER THE SIDE OF THE BUS to see exactly where he stood as he took his oath.* ***They were leaning into a lie.***

Why do we yearn to know exactly where George Washington stood? **Isn't historical accuracy just our memories becoming totalitarian on us?**

The study of history is often trying to convince us that there was only one story. We know that any anecdote has as many versions as people who witnessed it.

George Washington had no better idea why he was here than we do, and he was just as confused as we are. His most heroic moments happened on the nights he apologized to Martha for gawking at her girlfriends. *All the historical anecdotes of early American history that danced across this corner were extensions of* ***George Washington's NEED FOR A HUG.***

Directly across the street from George Washington's statue, is the **J. P. Morgan Guaranty Building.** On the Wall Street side, in the wall of bright, white limestone, one can still see pockmarks from the anarchist bomb that exploded here in 1920. It is still presumed that the anarchists attacked J. P. Morgan's headquarters because they deemed him one of the significant ingredients of World War One.

Let's walk north, past George Washington's statue, up the tiny street called **Nassau Street**. As we cross Wall Street, look off to the right. This is the full extent of this infamous street. Narrow—it was originally designed for horse carriages. About five or six blocks long with enormous buildings crammed together, ***Wall Street*** *is what* ***Brunelleschi****, the* ***Renaissance architect*** *who discovered perspective, envisioned as he* ***breathed his last breath***. From this corner, we are viewing the final breathless vision of that visionary.

Nassau Street is named after the royal family of the Netherlands and is an example of how some of the streets of Lower Manhattan still have their original Dutch names. Dutch, as a language, would leave its mark on American English in important places. The word "yacht," for instance, and the word "cookie." The British say "biscuit." If it weren't for the slight Dutch imperialism that went down on these streets, it is possible that **Cookie Monster** would have been chasing down biscuits his whole life.

The next corner is **Pine Street** and to the left is the enormous glass and aluminum **Chase Manhattan Bank Building**, approximately sixty stories high. The building houses the world's largest bank vault. It is five floors below ground and holds billions of dollars in "securities" and a few million dollars of actual cash. The building rings with bigness. Big money, big plaza, big people with big ideas on the topics of themselves and their place in the world. The whole bank is named after **Salmon Chase** who founded the current national banking system and its currency as secretary of the treasury under Abraham Lincoln.

But perhaps biggest of all, bigger than the personalities and even the building itself, and bigger than the billions of "securities" hanging out in the vault and even bigger than those securities' feelings of security, are the French businessman-turned-sculptor Jean Dubuffet's sculptural sixty-foot magic mushrooms sprouting out of the Chase Manhattan Plaza.

The simple visual truth lies before us as we stand on this astonishing monumental Financial District plaza—we are standing in the shadow of enormous **mushrooms.**

The Mayans called the mushroom *"FLESH OF THE GODS."* Their calendar, divided into five epochs, ends altogether on December 22, 2012. We are living in the time they termed the final epoch of human life on this planet. If we could return to Chichén Itzá and stand with the Mayans of two thousand years ago, and explain to them that we are actually alive on a city plaza in the middle of New York City in the last moments of their fifth epoch, their reply, translated from the Mayan, would sound like this: "Wow!"

Mushrooms are a tour guide in the landmark of irrationality. They are emissaries of the Earth guiding us across the incomprehensible, across the cliffsides of beyond belief.

Stand with me on this city plaza and watch the businessmen and other associates of commerce, dressed up in their appropriate wardrobes, pass back and forth, ignoring the sixty-foot mushrooms.

The mushrooms have come here to the Financial District because it is a place of NO SURRENDER.

It is a place where success is a measurement of the effective use of one's selfishness instead of the effective use of one's selflessness. This is a symptom of sullenness and of taking life too seriously. This leads to the attitude that everyone is here to protect us from ourselves. The mushrooms turn these tormented illusions into Silly Putty.

*For now, the **giant MUSHROOMS** stand here silently watching people lose sight of the fact that **reality is an u n f o l d i n g miracle*** as they commit themselves to competitive behavior.

Competition is the act of seeking an exit from your life. It is to be building a self with builders other than self. It is spending the day focusing attention on the opinions and actions of everyone else instead of concentrating on one's own struggle.

The entire idea of a **business** is to create a scheme where we feel justified in avoiding our own struggle. There we have bosses whose problems are considered more important than our own all day, every day. If "successful," we then become bosses who can delineate our struggle to the next generation.

As we walk away from the Chase Manhattan Plaza, toward Broadway, turn around and view the giant mushrooms and the pedestrians from a distance. The entire vision of tiny people wrapped up in their own dramas while being dwarfed by huge mushrooms is a microcosmic diorama of what is going on worldwide right now. According to prophets, gurus, the high-minded and courageous, and shamans, this planet has just now exited the two-thousand-year astrological alignment called the Age of Pisces and is now entering the **Age of Aquarius.** *It is time for us to give ourselves to the **UNKNOWN**, instead of expending all of our **life energy** demanding that **we know**.*

When we return to **Broadway**, take a left. At the corner of Wall and Broadway is the large brown church called **Trinity Church**. Trinity Church is actually the third church on this site. The church was originally chartered by King William the Third in 1697. Queen Anne granted the land in 1705 and this version was constructed in 1846. Queen Elizabeth, when she visited

New York in the twentieth century, stopped by Trinity Church and a plaque on the floor at the entrance of the church commemorates that Anglican landmark in time. In its initial incarnation, Trinity Church is the tallest structure of New York City's skyline.

Trinity Church's cemetery is a hall of fame. The hedge stones, older than the current church standing among them, crumble with mystery, early American genius and its insanity. **Robert Fulton**, inventor of the steamboat; **Albert Gallatin**, secretary of the treasury under Thomas Jefferson; **William Bradford**, the curator of the first printing press in America; **Captain James Lawrence**, a naval commander victorious in the permanent seas of vivacity when he spoke his dying command, "Don't give up the ship!" The Gothic spire that looks like the top of a buried church is a memorial to soldiers of the American Revolution who died as prisoners on Liberty Street.

Alexander Hamilton, secretary of the treasury under George Washington, co-author of the *Federalist* papers, and one of the founding fathers of the United States of America is buried next to his wife, **Eliza**, on the south side of the burial grounds. Hamilton, as a New Yorker, knew that Thomas Jefferson's Virginian vision of America as an agrarian nation was off. He knew America was destined to be a manufacturing nation. He founded the **Bank of New York** in 1784, the oldest commercial bank in the United States. The bank's current headquarters is on the corner of Wall Street and William Street.

Today, Alexander Hamilton's grave sits proudly next to a *shoe outlet*. This simple fact is proof that he was right.

Hamilton was killed in a pistol duel that occurred between him and **Aaron Burr** in Weehawken, New Jersey, in 1804. Burr, described by Abigail Adams as "the most insidious man of his generation," had founded the second major bank of the city called, the **Manhattan Company**. Their duel was actually a duel between banks and **the founding father's death was a heroic example of a CLASSIC CORPORATE TAKEOVER.**

Outside the gate of Trinity Church, we proceed down Broadway, considered to be one of the longest roads of the world. We are descending toward its absolute genesis.

At **39 Broadway**, note the small plaque that marks this address as the second White House of American history. This is where George Washington lived for six months in his first term as president of the United States. Though the house is long erased and replaced by a large commercial building, the cool energy of Washington's late-night contemplations still pervades.

At **26 Broadway** is the former **Standard Oil Building**, the corporate headquarters of John D. Rockefeller's Standard Oil Company. Rockefeller's famous quip **"Do unto others before they do it to you"** could be the epitaph inscripted across our intimacy's gravestone.

At **25 Broadway** is the former **Cunard Building.** Cunard was/is the major ocean-liner company whose first voyage between New York and England happened in 1840. The entire architecture is a vibratory reminiscence and a tactile ornament from the days when people would take stylish weeklong journeys across the Atlantic Ocean. Ships filled with piles of steaks, vats of wine, and fine delicacies would sail on the open seas as women's breasts in evening gowns swayed first port side then starboard side. The Renaissance façade suddenly sprouts a colonnade, the interior nautical vestibule flowing with the rhythm of an ocean, and flows into a great hall where the climax of an ocean liner vaults into revelries of great aquatic cruisers.

I often stand outside this building *thinking of Magellan*. I completely identify with him. The major decision of his life was whether to go with or against the wind.

MAGELLAN–the major decision of a discoverer's life is whether to go ***WITH or AGAINST the WIND.***

The oval-shaped park currently crowned by the statue of an enormous, charging bull is **Bowling Green Park.** This was, as we learned earlier, New York City's first park. In 1771, a statue of King George the Third of England was erected in Bowling Green and stood where the central fountain currently flows, quietly associating with the mythological metaphoric meaning of water as the unconscious. After the public reading of the Declaration of Independence on July 18, 1776, angry colonists rampaged through the streets and had a fun carnage with the King George statue. **(For more about Bowling Green Park, refer to "A Tour of the Statue of Liberty: Stay Free!")**

The ornate **U.S. Custom House** designed by **Cass Gilbert** stands behind the Bowling Green oval. Today it is the **National Museum of the American Indian.** The alive beaux arts architecture of the building, once commited to the commercial responsibilities of a busy trading harbor, now houses a monumental collection of Native American art.

The entire complex is a bizarre extended thought, extending from the initial awkward handshake that took place between Peter Minuit and his Reckagawawanc counterpart.

As we look around the corner of the U.S. Custom House, down State Street, we will see the Peter Minuit Plaza where we began this possibility for intimacy in a landscape built to protect us from it.

We have completed one big circle. A circle of worries leading to further worrying, a circle of achievements ***that have never achieved enough—in other words, THE "AMERICAN DREAM."***

At the end of the circle, let us put aside Wall Street consciousness and see beyond the American dream just for a moment and recognize that the only thing we ever truly pay for in this world is a lack of generosity.

Intimacy is a direct experience. It is not a theory, it is not something to be documented, it cannot be photographed; intimacy must be felt. The ability to share our feelings with other people begins with us actually feeling the feeling.

Now, experience a moment of true intimacy.

Draw a picture of yourself.

A Tour of Washington Square Park and My Heart: Fear is Joy Paralyzed

Most people do not know there is an end to pain, but I have been there. It is the place where fear and desire lose their significance.

—Maharaj

Why did I move to Greenwich Village? Because it was there that I finally found a community of people who do nothing.

—Marcel Duchamps

Every time a want becomes a need, anywhere in the world a DESPAIR CRIES OUT, Greenwich Village is affected. It is one of the sensitive vortexes of the planet's body, which is easily bruised and easily tickled; it is an ongoing multilingual, connoisseurship on the topic of joy, and therefore, it is an erogenous zone of the Earth.

*

Greenwich Village—the backside of one of the Earth's earlobes.

*

When I sing the anthem of Greenwich Village I am singing songs of a neighborhood that grew up more around a feeling of euphoria than a group of perimeter fences. This is actually a musical where in Act One the city asks us the question: "Your **self-doubt is doubting you** right now, what are you going to do about it?" And, Act Two is our answer.

This mad intertwining of ancient Native American dirt paths are today the paved concrete streets of the West Village which mad radicals, cerebrally imprisoned intellects, cosmopolitan shamans, and poets in love pace up and down like ongoing den floors. Greenwich Village, originally a northwest corner of a large meadow area, is a temporary hunting ground for an assortment of Native American tribes.

Ladies and gentlemen, get the horses. Today we are touring a hunting ground. We will be on the hunt for the most unpredictable animal in the food chain: ourselves.

***Greenwich Village** is built upon the secret that we **bump** into our **ecstasy** on the other side of our **fears**.* It takes more energy to be afraid than it does to overcome fear. Actually, overcoming fear is energizing while negotiating with fear is enervating. Greenwich Village's streetlamps are lit by all the energy manufactured whenever we notice that our fears are begging us to overcome them.

When I whisper "Greenwich Village" I am whispering the secrets of creativity. When your fears run from you down the cobblestones of this village, you start to feel creative. Stimulation is just a reminder of who we really are. Creativity is our pursuit of our original exuberance, the exuberance that we came into the world with before it was taken out to an abandoned dockside and shot in a gangster-style assassination. The expressions on the infant's faces, as they sail across the horizons of our entire lives, are keeping the artists of Greenwich Village busy tonight.

Greenwich Village is also a place crafted by the survivors of plague. The population grew here in direct ratio with the epidemics of cholera, typhus, and malaria spreading throughout the Lower East Side. Those who could afford it moved to these hills and dales that overlook the Hudson River in a heavenly cleansing ventilation.

This is also a radical occurrence called "Greenwich Village" where the infrastructures of our sanity are blown over by winds of our own blowing. *Revolution is our lives as movie stars. Radicalization is turning your vision of "limitlessness" into "limited" and moving onto the next "limitlessnessnessNESSnessnessnessssssnneessnessnessNeSsNESsneSsnneesss."*

Damn it, Simone-Mourning-Natasha! Greenwich Village is crying out to you tonight, "Balance is a cop-out!" Natasha-Mourning-Simone, listen to the story of Greenwich Village and be affirmed in your sanity! As a great Greenwich Village cruisader once proclaimed, "Those who can't hear the music must think the dancers mad." Natasha-Mopping-the-Dirty-Floors-with-Simone, if you ask me what your redemption has to do with the story of Greenwich Village I will answer, "Everything!"

Welcome to the landmark of neurotic genius!

WE BEGIN AT WASHINGTON SQUARE NORTH—IN FRONT OF THE WASHINGTON SQUARE ARCH—THE VERY BEGINNING OF FIFTH AVENUE:

When one first looks upon **Washington Square Park**, one is faced with the existential question: "What constitutes a park?" What percentage of green grass must cover the area and how much calm must be in the air for a plot of ground to be considered a park?

We are standing on the perimeter of the most prestigious aristocratic neighborhood of the mid-nineteenth century in the United States. Washington Square Park was then a private park enclosed by a large, black, wrought-iron gate, its keys held by the aristocrats living in the Greek Revival row houses that surround the park. The Greek Revivalist gesture found here would spread across America. The Greek Revivalist attitude and look was a perfectly aloof, polite sample of Grecian technology. Americans would do the same with Athenian democracy.

The **Washington Square Arch** is a marble exhibition of lust lasciviously proud.

The Washington Square Arch— *A MARBLE EXHIBITION OF LUST* *LASCIVIOUSLY PROUD.*

Stanford White, one of the single most influential architects of New York City's architectural heritage, designed this arch. Stanford White was assassinated. You know you are a good and influential architect if someone goes to the trouble of assassinating you. It means you are successfully impacting the population with your taste and someone else is willing to put his life on the line to put a stop to it.

Actually, *to be assassinated for one's tastes is one of the great compliments a life can receive.*

White was assassinated for a great, heterosexual reason. He was killed over a woman. He had carried on an affair with a sixteen-year-old girl named **Evelyn Nesbitt.** At the age of nineteen, Nesbitt married an uptight Pittsburgh aristocrat named **Harry K. Thaw.** Thaw could not tolerate the thought that White had known Nesbitt biblically before him. In a depraved, jealous rage, Thaw walked up to Stanford White during the intermission of a stage play that has never ended. This all happens on the roof garden of the **second Madison Square Garden** **(see "We Do Not Fear Death As Much As We Fear Immortality: Madison Square Park")**, a mad hyperbolic mix of High Spanish Renaissance architecture and sports arena. Thaw, standing on a structure and in a karmic unfolding that were both architected by Stanford White, shoots the architect up close three times and thus punctuates one of the most illustrious careers New York City has ever seen.

Lurid accounts of White's lasciviousness rampaged through the newspapers in the aftermath of the murder. Stories were published about his "**velvet swing**" that he used for kinky copulation in the apartment he had designed for himself in Madison Square Garden's central tower.

Today it is clear that his greatest architectural design happened at his friend's bachelor party. ***Stanford White*** *created the* ***first large birthday cake*** *ever to be wheeled into a room full of men and* ***exploded*** *by a* ***stripper.*** When that very first stripper leaped out of that very first cake, she leaped into a world where maidservants were ordered to cover the legs of furniture for fear that the children might be given lewd thoughts. This time period is called the **Gilded Age.** It was a time of irrepressibly repressed repression protecting itself with purposeful obliviousness, etiquette, and ostentatiousness.

If we think the Victorian era was so long ago we should study the matter more carefully. The Victorians were only four generations ago and their weirdness and repressiveness on the topic of sex is the same as our weirdness and repressiveness toward our minds. We are "Victorians of the mind" just as much as Stanford White's generation were Victorians of the body.

Therefore, the thought of Stanford White gets me hot. He was an avaricious appreciator of beauty, who had the courage to, once in a while, exhibit the fact that he was thrilled to be alive, whether that exhibition found personification through his lust conspiracies with feminine flesh or his marble edifices. This exhibition of thrill made him an unconscious public enemy who was certain to be squashed by a world orchestrated by self-loathing and the industrial invention of depression.

Depression is most certainly an invention. Civilization helped us invent depression so that our interpretation of civilization would be an upside-down, demoralized conclusion that, as an event, is heaven sent. The conviction that we need to be tamed is the part of us that invented depression. The part of ourselves that still weeps when a wild horse gets tamed is the part of us that knows that doubt is dream and foreplay is autobiography and this is the part of ourselves that is too busy dreaming and having foreplay to have doubt or autobiography.

Depression is the part of us that has already died, and so has no problem with being civilized.

In 1889, Stanford White is given a commission to construct a monument that will stand at the very beginning of the main vein of his world, Fifth Avenue. **Millionaire's Row**, as Fifth Avenue was known, is just as much a place to be seen as it is a place to live. The city, a great architect of reality, asks Stanford White to design a monument celebrating the centennial of George Washington's oath of office as the first president of the United States, which took place at Wall Street and Broad on April 30, 1789. The Bastille in Paris would fall only ten weeks later.

I prefer to hang out with people who are either on their way to the Bastille or who have just come back. I figure this is an incredible time to be alive, and I'm here to play ball. So I hang out on the road where people travel to and from revolutions.

The greatest ***REVOLUTIONARY ACT*** *of all is* ***GETTING OUT OF BED in the morning.*** All revolutions began with people getting out of bed in the morning.

Stanford White is going to decorate one of the prominent spots in the world that constructed him and all of his constructions, a world where Stanford White has been made to feel insane whenever he enjoyed himself too much. He is a soldier of bliss lost deep behind enemy lines, strutting.

He chooses an ancient symbol—the triumphal arch. Roman legions would build these after conquering a town. The arch would bestride the entrance of their new conquest, so that the army could march through it, consummating their triumph between a twin pair of sprawled thighs. Today, this arch is a shapely invitation for us to march.

When we look up Fifth Avenue through the orifice of this arch, we can clearly see Fifth Avenue being born. Fifth Avenue is kicking and screaming as it emanates continually from this feminine opening. ***FIFTH AVENUE is a gigantic baby.*** "Civilization is enforced infantilism." (**For more about civilization as enforced infantilism, refer to "A Tour of the Statue of Liberty: Stay Free!"**)

The Parks Department often has reasons to put a fence around this triumphal arch. It is clearly a chastity belt clamped around the massive opening. Is it an attempt to blockade fertility or triumph? Which do you think the city administration is more afraid of?

George Washington appears all over the arch and is being used by the architect for his own personal healing. On bright, sunny, horny days the **Washington Square Arch** can be heard admitting that it ***doesn't know who George Washington is.*** The Washington Square Arch proclaims nothing about vague, nationalistic liberty, but instead, just like the park of its namesake, is an event announcing the most intimate personal freedoms. The arch is screaming up this prominent avenue, "I am thrilled to be alive!" and "What's your phone number, baby?!"

Stand with the triumphal arch for a moment and stare out at Fifth Avenue. Fifth Avenue stares back at you. Examine whatever sensations you are feeling. (It's all right not to feel triumphant.)

Note the cascades of **pigeons** flying across the horizon. These birds have witnessed the entire story of Washington Square Park. The pigeons are teachers. Sages living among us to prove that anything and anybody can be adored. In this current consciousness, New Yorkers are very critical of the pigeon. Pigeons are often described as "flying rats" and "dirty birds." The pigeons will transform into the most beautiful birds any of us have ever seen the moment they are fully appreciated.

The reason NEW YORKERS criticize PIGEONS is because they have too much in common with them. The similarities are eerie. Notice how the pigeon organizes his entire day around the seeking of crumbs. The pigeon is greatly dexterous only when he needs to be. They are fast enough to evade an automobile coming right at them at forty miles per hour, only to reland on the sidewalk with a somber, infinite waddle that has no destination in sight.

Whenever a New Yorker has a moment of self-consciousness, somewhere a pigeon is born.

Pigeons are also walking examples of divinity. "Divinity is when no one fears you and you fear no one."

On this tour of our fears overcome, the pigeon represents salvation.

As we enter the park itself, feel yourself wading into the sexy waters of a theoretical gene pool. As we walk toward the central fountain, watch and feel all the fantastic, informal and formal, crazed and lucid, singing and screaming attempts to get your attention. This park is famous for its street performers. We are all street performers, but in Washington Square Park, it is obvious that some street performers are more aware of the performance.

The system of gimmicks we initiate in order to enter each other's psyches, I call *shticking.* A discussion of shticking is the study of spotlighting agendas and detaching from them, understanding that the gimmicks and role-playing that emanate from our desire is great theater. **To shtick is to embrace the socialization at hand. When we shtick we are playing society's conditioning like an instrument.**

Washington Square Park is one of the great shticking parlors of this vain world. In this culture "to be is to be perceived." "Persona is existence!" is the daily declaration of the superficial. A good shtick is an earnestness traveling in disguise. It is an ennobled attempt at attention. A good shticker is someone who understands that attention is something we all have for one reason and one reason only: to give to each other.

A bad shtick is pulled by the person who no longer has an agenda; the agenda has the person. A bad shtick is an unoriginal attempt to satisfy biology and its demands. **Many studly men who score with a lot of women are pulling bad shticks, while many good shticks lead to SEXUAL REJECTION.** This is further proof that civilization is doomed.

We will be veering to the left of the central fountain and as we do note all the shticks going on around you and try to decide for yourself which shticks you think are good and which shticks you think are bad.

As we continue to walk in a straight line from the eastern side of the fountain, we see a near-distant statue of a man wielding a sword. It is a statue of **Garibaldi**—the Italian revolutionary.

You might be asking—and it is a perfectly good, which is to say valid, question to ask—"Why Garibaldi?"

I am a tour guide. I do not speak in facts or logical paradigms or intellectualization. ***I speak in explosions. I promote thinking and feeling on the topic of ourselves.*** And so, I do not know why or how Garibaldi comes to be here before us. I can offer a few possible explanations. I am not dogmatic about any of them. Any explanation, whether it is valid or not, has within it the instruments of our freedom. Let each hypothetical lead to rhetorical questions that cause your courage to stand up for itself.

The first possibility of why, perhaps, Garibaldi is here is that he lived for a few years on Staten Island. This was in the years before his return to Italy when he led Victor Emmanuel's army to triumph after triumph resulting in the **Italian Unification of 1871.**

So it might be valid to say he is a New Yorker.

The word "New Yorker" is a great oxymoron. How can such an international place filled with so many different perspectives and worldviews believe that its citizenship could be described by three syllables? The term "New Yorker" is a term. A term is a series of words meant to help move the afternoon along.

If someone raised a gun to my head and asked me what a New Yorker is (and that has happened), I would say a New Yorker is someone who has come to this place *to run wild with their healing*. A soul that has come to this convention of souls to pursue self. It is the pursuit that makes the New Yorker.

Escape From New York, the great action-thriller, futuristic movie by John Carpenter, is a line description of the great New Yorker. In the film's plot, it's 2012 and **Manhattan is a GIGANTIC HIGH-SECURITY PRISON** and all the prisoners of America are dumped onto the island and left to live among themselves. Civilization has not existed on Manhattan for many years when Air Force One, the airplane carrying the president of the United States, crashes and jettisons the president safely onto 42nd Street. The world is precariously nearing Armageddon and the president is carrying a cassette in his jacket pocket that will save the world.

Snake Plitsken, played by **Kurt Russell,** is a mercenary who wears an eye patch and is somehow in New Jersey being told by federal agents that he has to go into mad Manhattan's society, find the president, and get him out. As they give Plitsken these instructions, they stick a needle into his arm. When he asks them what they just shot him up with they explain it is a capsule of poison they implanted in his bloodstream that will implode in his system in exactly twenty-four hours. Only they can remove the capsule, and they will only remove the poison when he brings back the president. He has twenty-four hours to complete his mission otherwise he is a dead man.

In this moment, Plitsken is a New Yorker. He comes to this island to face a major mission of a lifetime and visions of his self-annihilation and he must heal himself. ***Manhattan*** *is* ***less*** *a* ***destination*** *and* ***more*** *an ongoing* ***exam.***

Fate just keeps tossing exams at us, and as we pass them, they get harder and harder.

Rocker **David Lee Roth**, in his autobiography, *Crazy from the Heat*, tells the story about the first time his father drove him into Greenwich Village. Roth was six years old and his favorite thing in the world: magazines. He was fascinated by the idea of a magazine and he was interested in all kinds. When he got out of his father's car on Thompson Street, he was faced with a newsstand. On one wall of the newsstand hung more magazines than he had ever conceived possible.

In this moment, Roth is a New Yorker. *He is faced with his favorite thing and his favorite thing is being presented to him in a numberless momentousness that is BLOWING HIS MIND.* Any vision of infinity he had has been instantly dwarfed.

And so, perhaps Garibaldi is here because he is a New Yorker.

Another reason why Garibaldi might be standing in Washington Square Park is that he was Italian. Due to the Italian Unification that Garibaldi consummated, millions of Italian peasants who had been contained to the Italian peninsula and their poverty there were suddenly given the opportunity to leave. Three million Italians land in the Lower East Side of Manhattan (**refer to "A Tour of the Lower East Side: You Are a Better Party Than Any Party Ever"**) between 1871 and 1920. **The Lower East Side is the most populated patch of Earth at that time, probably one-and-a-half times the population density of Bombay, India.**

All these Italians start pouring out of the overcrowded Lower East Side into Greenwich Village, bringing ancient persecutions and great pizza.

These Italians are at play in this oxygen because of Garibaldi's work. Perhaps that is why some of them wanted him represented here.

A third somewhat reason as to why, maybe, Garibaldi is standing in Washington Square Park is because he is a revolutionary.

How many times, drunken and confused, did **Thomas Paine** traipse across this very ground we're standing on as he went home to write *Common Sense* and *Crisis*, two of the most influential political pamphlets of all time? George Washington and those other militaristic studs were fighting a war over an issue—taxation without representation. It took a **neurotic genius named THOMAS PAINE** to explain to them that it was a ***REVOLUTION.***

How many times, drunken and confused and fighting for paganism, did **Jack Reed** wander across this pavement as he went to a salon room above a West 3rd Street bar to write *Ten Days That Shook the World.* This was his editorial account of the Russian Revolution that landed his corpse in the Kremlin wall—the first and only American to be buried in the Kremlin wall.

How many times, not so drunk and not very confused, did **Samuel Gompers** walk across this park, selling cigars one at a time. He went on to found the American Federation of Labor. His life was one long union banner waving in an ever-polluted wind of American postindustrialization and selfishness.

We are standing, right now, amid the ghosts involved with the very first out-loud, exhibitionistic labor riot of American history, the **Stonecutter's Rebellion.** The large white building skirting the eastern edge of the park is the second main building of New York University and in 1831 this plot of land was the site of the first main building's construction. New York University replaces the local freelance stonecutters and hires free prison labor to dress the marble for their central building.

The stonecutters come back with brickbats and rage and start busting up the mantelpieces and other apparatus used for the purpose of building. They attempt to destroy what they had until recently been creating. This is the initial knee-jerk reaction laborers had to their first taste of the Industrial Revolution. Eventually, the National Guard is called in and **THE STONECUTTERS WERE BEATEN UP AND HUMILIATED.**

From here, we have a view of the top of the Washington Square Arch where **Marcel Duchamp and John Sloan**, representatives of the Dadaism movement and the Ashcan School of art, stood one night in 1912 and pronounced a revolution of the absurd. Absurdity is the revolution marching triumphantly through our hearts and minds every day.

And so another reason of why, perhaps, Garibaldi stands before us wielding a sword in this park is because he dared. **Daring** is the striptease of fear. To dare is to strip fear naked and bereft of all the ingenious disguises it takes on throughout the adventure of a day.

Daring is the *striptease of fear.*

As we move southwest toward the **Judson Church** in the distance, dare. Dare! Melt one of your basic beliefs into disbelief, overcome one of your main fears, and find a new relationship to reality by the time we get to the south side of the park.

The Judson Church is the gold tower with transparent crucifix atop it in the near distance. It is another classical structure designed by Stanford White. To the south, distantly, the **World Trade Center** once stood—the former tallest buildings of New York's skyline. The World Trade Center subway station was one of the great vista views of **morning and afternoon rush hour.** There was a flowing, mad river of escalators filled with people on every step in all directions for a couple of hours each weekday morning and afternoon. Two hundred thousand people worked in the World Trade Center daily. The buildings had their own zip code. **(For more on the World Trade Center, see "A Tour of the Statue of Liberty: Stay Free;" for more on rush hour see "The Midtown Rush Hour Tour.")**

Also, to the south, closer but out of sight, palpably pulsating the ground upon which we stand is **Bleecker Street.** If all the streets of Greenwich Village were sisters, this is ***the sister who moved to the big city and got her own ideas.*** Bleecker Street is a highly commercialized street today with a nightclub in the middle of it called "Life." Night people wait in line to see if they are on the guest list to get into life. This is the line I stand in most of the time.

Washington Square South is the street stretching itself out underneath our feet. It is famous for being a stretch of affordable row houses and hotels, whose rents were kept low by landlords who supported the artists living in their midst. A landlord keeping rents low for irrational, even artistic reasons in New York City is the most subversive action possible in a city that is an encapsulated capitalistic experiment hell-bent at all times on seeking new real estate. New York City's history runs the same course as our saliva. It is wondrous and obviously simultaneous that ***much of American literature and American culture*** **were crafted under the protection of** ***LANDLORDS who had*****, according to New York City,** ***gone insane.***

I remember how I felt the first time I stood on this spot and someone pointed to the corner of La Guardia and Washington Square South and told me that *The Red Badge of Courage* was written there. I felt the ceremony of Eugene O'Neill's typewriter ringing out from one of these windows overlooking the park, and I heard Edgar Allen Poe reading "The Raven" out loud for the first time—which he did do on West 3rd Street not that long ago, but long enough now that it seems like a dream.

The Judson Church stands as another example of Stanford White's psyche. If Ralph Waldo Emerson were on this tour, I think he would be asking us as well as Stanford White, "Why are we recapitulating High Italian Renaissance architecture on a new square, in a new city, in a new land with infinite possibility in front of us? What are we going to learn from Italian history other than suicide and good pasta?" Faced with this view of Judson Church, ***I think Emerson would be moved to exclaim, "We are new! So new it's 'I knew' but no, you did not know*** and you still have no idea how new this could be. The human race is a permanent virgin and we are newer than the newest car driven to its new home by the proudest father. That's how new we are!"

Stanford White would answer, "***Look, Emerson, cut me some slack.*** Life and architecture work in cycles. Circling is what we mainly do. Even the Renaissance was rebirth and new ideas are only old ideas that have matured." Commenting on this specific choice, I think White would say, "I like my two classical forms on either side of this park. Depending on where you stand, depending on where the sun is shining, this park becomes a plaza in a twelfth-century Italian village or the ancient Roman Forum." I think White would also proclaim, "All the people in this park are standing between two panting, longing lovers—the archway's cavernous opening and the church's tower. This park is foreplay!"

Let's go to the dog run.

It was during long meditations in the dog run that I became fully riveted to the knowledge that the human being is the only animal on the planet noticing that biological agenda and enjoying life are often two different situations, two different responsibilities, two different parties.

Take a moment here to get inside one of the human being's shoes and then try to get inside one of the dog's paws. Compare and contrast the experiences.

Before you turn around, let me just tell you that directly behind us as you face the dog run is a bust of **Alexander Holley**, the famous exploiter of the Bessamer process that made steel more practical.

Ignore this statue.

The cameras of our lives are in more direct intercourse with the present tense than we are whenever we view the tour as a series of photo opportunities spent at the feet of landmarks primped and shaped in the name of becoming picture-postcards. It's as if we do not bother to stop and appreciate beauty unless something constructive will come out of it, like a photograph or the memorialization of some trivial fact. When, actually, appreciating beauty for no reason at all is the key to enjoying life.

Don't allow the pedestal to demand your attention! Do not allow the pedestal to alert you to the fact that it stands there as a marker for your sudden attentiveness. Instead, look everywhere else where the unexpected is dancing all around you. **Don't blink! The reality unfolding around you is an *alive, throbbing* postcard** ceaselessly changing right before your eyes!

Let us go, you and I, to the northwest corner of the park where the eighteenth century awaits us.

On the way, if we look through the trees in a southwesterly direction, we can see the **chess circle** at another corner of the park. Russian masters and other high-rated chess players wait to play passing pedestrians at tables with chessboard tabletops. My **cousin Bruce** has been going to one such aged Russian master even though the man speaks no English and Bruce speaks no Russian. They meet there during the hours just after dawn and play a chess game that never ends. Bruce will make a move and the two will examine the infinite possibilities and ramifications of that one move in a theoretical movement of pieces invisible to the entire world except them. I asked Bruce how he and this aged master communicated so miraculously well without a common language. Bruce answered, in his own soft voice, "We descend from the same agony."

Cousin Bruce and a homeless Russian chess master share an infinite game invisible to the entire world except them and their common AGONY.

At the northwest corner, the oldest standing tree in Manhattan stands tall in front of us. Informally known as the "Hanging Tree," the enormous elm blossoms are the last eyewitnesses to a lost world. The tree is where "justice" was rendered two hundred years ago in New York City. Is this not *the loftiest EXECUTIONER you have ever seen?*

This was a convenient place to hang prisoners because before Washington Square Park was a private, aristocratic neighborhood and before this park was an Italian immigrant and creative Bohemia and before it was the central campus for the largest private university of the United States, this place was the potter's field of Lower Manhattan. This was the open ditch reserved for unidentified corpses, the corpses of slaves, diseased corpses, and corpses of dead prisoners.

The poltergeist energy emanating from below this park, every single breathless last breath and all that depraved death, has on a daily basis co-written this two hundred year drama called "Washington Square Park." The degradations done to each body, each mind, each soul has contributed wildly to the day-to-day events that have taken place in and around this park.

Right now, standing on this corner, we are four-and-a-half blocks from where **Mark Twain** moved right after his wife passed away. Twain moves at that time to West 10th Street a few doors down from **O'Henry**.

Undoubtedly, Edgar Allen Poe felt dizzy on this corner we are standing on.

We are breathing the same air **Henry James**, the novelist, breathed when he was born on the perimeter of this park, and we are dealing with the same neurosis **Edith Wharton** dealt with when she was "too intelligent to be fashionable," an aristocratic child experiencing aristocratic paralysis. She wrote *The House of Mirth* here, of course.

We are standing six blocks from where **Henry Miller** decides he hates New York forever and moves to Paris. Eight blocks from where **Willa Cather** felt depressed often and attempted to live. Four blocks from where **Sherwood Anderson** lived and from where **e. e. cummings** impregnated a woman and didn't know about it and from where **Theodore Dreiser** wrote *Sister Carrie* and then none of his friends would talk to him and he walked the streets every night drunk. We are four blocks from where **Hart Crane** lives and makes love to **García Lorca**, from where **Edward Albee** writes *The Zoo Story* and shows us that **alienation is just ourselves forgetting how great we are at *energizing* each other**, and from where **D. H. Lawrence** lived lasciviously.

We are two blocks from 14A Washington Mews, a studio where **Edward Hopper** painted, from where **John Dos Passos** wrote, and from there we are right across the street from 13 East 8th Street where **Thomas Wolfe** began *Look Homeward, Angel.*

Somewhere nearby, **Edna St. Vincent Millay** wrote poetry that is both pretty and beautiful as she apparently was. We stand two blocks from where **William Carlos Williams** became something else that depends upon a red wheelbarrow, from where *The Little Review* published James Joyce's *Ulysses* in installments and its editors were convicted of obscenity. We are rocking where **Bob Dylan** rocked when he resided on positively West 4th Street, and we are two blocks from where **Dylan Thomas** lost consciousness for the last time in the White Horse Tavern his famous last words, ***"I just had my sixteenth whiskey."***

We are a few blocks from where **Max Eastman** edits **The Masses**, a communist publication, in a refurbished plumber's shop, just a couple of blocks from where government officials handcuff and exile **Emma Goldman,** an early spokeswoman for contraception in American history whose opposition to America's participation in World War One unnerved the American government to the extent that it had her removed from the continent. When they loaded her onto the boat headed for Russia, she proclaimed to the press, **"THE MOST POWERFUL GOVERNMENT IN THE WORLD IS *AFRAID OF AN OLD WOMAN!"***

The **Triangle Shirtwaist Company** fire took place around the corner in 1911, horrifically burning over a hundred young women laborers alive. The awful image of young seamstresses strewn across the sidewalk of Greene Street transformed labor laws in America.

We are just around the corner from where **Hippolyte Havel** was simultaneously a short-order cook and an anarchist, just down the street from where **F. Scott Fitzgerald** chased his wife **Zelda** drunkenly through revolving doors that were invisible to everyone except them, just a couple of blocks from the Liberal Club on MacDougal Street where many individuals confused about their sexuality gathered nightly with plans to change the world.

We are three blocks from where **James Dean** posed for the famous photograph of himself in front of the Thompson Street newsstand. We are eight blocks from where **Herman Melville** lives Greenwich Village-impoverished near the river for the couple of years right before he writes *Moby Dick*. We are limping along the West Village sidewalks with **Washington Irving** as he realizes the plotline for "The Legend of Sleepy Hollow" and quietly condescends to the world. We are two blocks from Bleecker Street with **James Fenimore Cooper** and the confusion he felt in 1833 (and we recommend therapy), and we are just around the corner sharing a drink with **Norman Mailer**—it's the 1950s and he is just realizing that boxing agrees with his central nervous system.

Once we enter 1950s Greenwich Village, we enter a place becoming a center for **jazz.** Of course, Greenwich Village heard and deeply felt this music. Invented by the children of slaves, here is a group of instruments finding harmony together despite their differences and strong individualities. Jazz finds harmony when the instruments equally respect each other's contribution.

You can hear from here the improvisations of bebop in the wind. You can hear **Charlie Parker** playing standards in the name of personalizing them in **The Village Vanguard**, you can hear **Dizzy Gillepsie** recounting, with a trumpet, what a night in Tunisia sounded like in **The Blue Note**, you can hear **Max Roach** having a soft and hard conversation with his past as the conversation results in a drumroll, you can hear **John Coltrane** and that certain way he prayed to God, you can hear **Chet Baker** as he realizes, while singing a Gershwin tune, that he is going to get laid tonight.

We are three blocks from where **Arthur Miller** contemplated suicide and from where **Jim Morrison** still does. We are just down the street from where **Harry Chapin** realized his hunger was not being satisfied by food, and from where **Dorothy Parker** wrestles with alcoholism and the defeats of a lifetime, and fails. We are just down the street from **Walt Whitman** as he writes,

> I am with you . . . you men and women of future
> generations, hence . . . Brooklyn of ample hills was mine,
> I too bathed in the waters 'round Manhattan . . . New York
> women . . . I will die so that I may return to you . . .

Welcome to a landmark of neurotic genius.
You have been brought to this corner to realize your own . . .

A Tour of SoHo, or How to Render Sexual Frustration Obsolete

In a city, people are the nature.
—Doug Rhodes

To lust with just sex organs is **biology.** ***To lust with one's entire being is CRUISING.***

On the streets of SoHo today, we will get laid more than anywhere else we have ever been, whether we get an opportunity to touch anyone or not.

To produce one's own ORGASMS ANYWHERE AT ANYTIME is an ESSENTIAL SKILL in this **Age of Sexual Frustration**; SoHo is a perfect place to practice because it is filled with sex and sexiness in the most vicarious, unfertile way possible.

In SoHo, to be governed by the fear of engaging others is to be *cool.* To overcome the fear of engaging others is *not cool. Exclusivity* is the reigning religion of this district currently. Therefore, the most successful SoHo nightclub is the one denying entrance to the most people.

There are no traffic jams in SoHo: there are **TANTRIC ORGIES** with horns and exhaust.

Welcome to SoHo!

WE BEGIN AT BROADWAY AND CANAL:

Our journey into vicarious orgasm starts by looking south. We are standing on a bluff that hangs over the **Collect Pond**, the indigenous pool where water collected.

The Collect Pond is no longer visible because it is now submerged beneath the urbania in front of us. Drains in the basements of these buildings have pumps that are actively draining the Collect Pond right now. When these pumps stop pumping, the basements flood with the wet flowing of a pond held back from its natural expansiveness and osmosis for over a century.

The VICARIOUS ORGASM is *one* that *consumates* the ILLIMITABILITY *of our* LOVE and ENERGY. It is a plunging headfirst into the pools of our own liquidity and forgetting how to swim. The orgasm is manufactured by a dance of retention and explosion similiar to the retention and expansion the Collect Pond experiences, similiar in rhythm to the undulations of the enormous adrenal gland expressing itself in front of us, also known as **Canal Street**.

Canal Street, was/is originally a canal. It was designed to channel some of the Collect Pond's water into the East River, an appendage of the Atlantic Ocean. This canal was a vein that coursed with all the different types of water that flow in and around the island: *SALT WATER, sweet water,* ***polluted water,*** **DRINKING WATER, *SEWAGE*** *water, and waters that flow in the name of BATHING BEAUTIFUL,* ***NAKED, young women and VIRILE young men.***

Canal Street and ourselves have much in common. We are both essentially water in the middle of experiencing different themes of thirst. Thirst affects our breathing patterns. **Feel the rhythm of Canal Street's breathing and compare it to your own. Cruise the desperate longing publicly shared between bargains and bargain hunters, between pedestrians and automobiles, between electrical supply stores *and* electricians.** Canal Street is filled with symbiotic relationships, and it is here that the city is showing us that symbiosis is, most of all, a converging of rhythms.

The breath we breathe is the life energy of ourselves flowing through the body, and your next breath is the only thing truly urgent in your life. The Chinese call this *chi* and the Hindus call this *prahna*, but you call it whatever you like.

Concentrate on your breath. Feel the breath fill your stomach and then empty out of your stomach. Breathe out all the energy of your sexual maladjustments. Breathe in all the love you can detect coming to you from the outside world, no matter how little that amount might be.

As we turn and look north along Broadway, recognize officially, as you twist your torso, that the **thorasic diaphragm** in the chest is only one of several diaphragms in your body. The pelvic diaphragm is the diaphragm at the bottom of the body's pelvic floor and is an associate of the **uro-genital diaphragm** that sits atop the **perineum**, which is the point midway between the sex organ and the anus. ***The PELVIC DIAPHRAGM has gone unidentified by Western medicine because* Western medicine is AFRAID of it.** These two diaphragms, the lowest in the body, serve as the navigational devices to the powerful jet engine you have between your legs; if you are a woman, you can consider your whole body a jet engine.

Standing on Broadway, notice again this boulevard of irrationality embedded within the rational grid plan of New York City. It is an excellent place to get in touch with the perineum. ***Lack of contact with the perineum led to the MAJOR RIOT of New York City's history, which took place here in 1863.*** As I now flow into a discussion of the **Draft Riots of 1863**, increase the depth of the breaths, and with each inhalation fill your stomach with air, flex the stomach muscles, and push the air down into the pelvic region. Once the life energy is in your pelvic region, flex the pelvic diaphragm, sense the presence of your perineum, and force the energy into your genitals and anus. As you exhale, feel the breath rise up your spinal cord. Do not allow this next historicism to distract you; instead recognize that some of the feelings you are capable of feeling right now were important events leading to the Draft Riots of 1863.

The riots begin when **Abraham Lincoln** ordered the conscription of New York City's men into the Union army. At that time, and especially in this district, the majority of New York City's men were immigrants working sixteen-hour days in these former factories for minimum wage. These men were mostly of German and Irish descent, and were all fresh to the United States. They had no interest in America's civil war and they had even less interest in dying in it.

Inhale.

New York City was, in fact, very close to seceding from the Union along with the Southern states because the majority of the population was terrified and completely opposed to the notion of freeing slaves. For New York City's men, free slaves meant the incoming migration of a new labor force even more subjugated, which is to say, even more desperate for work. Free slaves would be willing to work for even cheaper wages than they were.

Fernando Wood, the New York mayor who was arrested on

the steps of City Hall for being a renegade dictator, made a major political comeback as the leader of the secessionist movement. New York City came very close to seceding from the Union along with the Southern states during the American Civil War. **Push the breath downward into the pelvic region and *flex*.**

To raise the stakes further, city officials proclaimed that with a three-hundred-dollar donation a man could be exempted from the draft. This was an unrealistic option for the laborers of SoHo, and the 4th Ward in general, and the Irish populations of Five Points and Hell's Kitchen, but it was not an unlikely choice for those living uptown.

The morning the draft offices opened they went up in flames, all of them, instant altars to **Mars**, the God of War. In refusing to fight in a combat situation, New Yorkers invented their own form of combat. Eighty thousand participants collaborated in five days of rampage that could, in every sense, be termed a civil war. ***Push your tongue to the roof of your mouth and as you send the life energy from your genitals up your spine, start to feel a sensation on the backside of your tongue.*** This is the thoroughfare that we will use to transport the orgasmic vibration produced by the second chakra to the body and the brain. Many practitioners of the vicarious orgasm have stated that once you have orgasms in the brain you never go back.

City officials were nervous about the loyalty of the police department and that morning were eyeing their police officers with suspicion. It was probably the same expression on the faces of Roman praetors when they served their generals fine wine and women the night before battle.

The police department was nearly 100 percent Irish, as were most of the rioters, and when city officials commanded the police to overwhelm a barricade that had been set up by Irish residents of Hell's Kitchen at 54th Street and Eighth Avenue, the city officials were actually waiting to see if this miniature civil war born of the larger Civil War would be consumated. Two hundred died that day in Hell's Kitchen as Irishman killed Irishman.

Eventually, the Draft Riots of 1863 would produce three thousand fatalities over five days. By the fifth day, the topic of the draft had been exasperated long before, and ***the riot was just an unfocused rage winding down, as all tragedies do, INTO FARCE.***

Look at the parking lot on the northwest corner of **Grand Street and Broadway**, which was one of the early sites of the **Lord & Taylor Department Store**, the oldest extant department store of Manhattan. Now the store is located on 39th Street and Fifth Avenue, the same corner where an orphanage of young black children sat in 1863 before it was burned to the ground in the Draft Riots. **(Also, refer to "A Tour of Ladies Mile: Women Are Life.")**

In 1863, the mezzanine lobby area of this Lord & Taylor's was used as a temporary hospital during the riots. Employees were armed with weapons so that they could, if need be, protect themselves and the store from *BAD* **FASHION** *CHOICES*.

When the smoke of the Draft Riots cleared, most of the men who had rioted end up fighting and dying in the American Civil War anyway. At Cold Harbor, **Ulysses S. Grant** misjudged the Confederate guns and lost much of New York City's generation of young men in the first five minutes of battle.

Henry Miller once said, while wading in a swimming pool, ***"Americans are warm and FEROCIOUS all at once."***

The most important riots and battlefields are happening inside of us right now. ***Cruise and anti-Cruise,*** *this is an eternal* **battlefield** *cascading across our own stomach lining.* Joy and joylessness, victory on this battlefield is the achievement of **self-love.**

Self-love is MASTURBATION on a GALACTIC level. It exhibits itself lewdly and with self-grandiosity every time we refuse to tolerate violence in our lives. Violence is anti-self-love, unhappiness acting out in the name of unhappiness; an ongoing forgetting that happiness is a possibility. **(Also, refer to "Wall Street: The Story of What Happened to Our Intimacy.")**

If my discussion of the Draft Riots is making you feel really hot right now, you are tapping into the fact that the sexy physical sensations you can cause yourself to feel while standing on this sidewalk are more historically accurate than a three-hundred-page, microscopic, academic study of the topic.

I'm sure this discussion of the ***Draft Riots*** has invented a new form of ***disco*** somewhere and is causing ***young people to move their hips*** in a whole new way.

I hope your own riots are raging out and are ready to concentrate their focus on the **Haughwout Building**.

On the northeast corner of **Broadway and Broome**, the recently white-painted, cast-iron building is the Haughwout Building. It is known as the **"Parthenon of Cast Iron Architecture"** and is one of the few cast-iron examples that predates the American Civil War.

The cast-iron architecture for which SoHo is famous was invented in England when architects successfully heated pig iron to its melting point and thus found that the iron could be made malleable while maintaining its full carbon content, and therefore, its strength.

Cast iron became popular in New York City's architecture after the great fires of of 1835 and 1845 when, on each occassion, hundreds of buildings were lost in a single evening. The architects were attempting to build with materials that were not flammable, materials that could not be inundated by flame and fire, or at least ones that refused to be affected by drastic heat and smoke. Of course, **CAST IRON in its superficial components and on good days appears to be nonflammable but upon closer inspection, like so many people I know, is more *incendiary* than it might seem.**

CAST IRON *is the FLESH OF TRANSITION,* and where there is transition there is life. It is the material of opulent decadent meticulousness and the material of stark hard industralization, simultaneous.

The tight rhythmic arches of the Haughwout Building are supported by twin Corinthian columns, which repeat with precision throughout. The façade is an industrial Palladian, textural escapade. It looks like a High Renaissance palace and a prefabricated, Industrial Revolution factory all at once. Cast iron is here stretched across epochs when the time of smooth became the sweating of now.

As we caress the Haughwout Building with our physical senses **let us take a moment to recognize that our physical senses are liberators and INCARCERATORS.** Our eyes are daring us to see beyond them, our ears dare us to hear everything at once, our ability to touch is not an end but a means. I am standing here right now in front of the Haughwout Building as an elusive masturbator, senselessly running through forests of myself as I make love to the precise cornice line of this façade, I am naked before the world. ***SQUEEZE together the muscles around your SEX ORGANS, your ANUS, and your ABDOMINALS.*** *Yoga practitioners all over the world call this* ***a root lock.*** Squeeze the lower three chakras all at once and force the energy up into the higher chakras. The root lock turns your entire body into a kiss between your higher and lower energy centers. Repeat this posture until you feel like a gigantic kiss that has learned the secret of locomotion. Keep breathing.

The last time I stood in front of the Haughwout Building I was giving a walking tour and a man in the group, looking up at the façade, asked, "Why did they make it so beautiful? Why didn't they just build a building that would stand?" I answered, "They made the building beautiful because they felt beautiful."

The entire group looked at me as if I was insane.

Conformity is the belief that procreation, and the obligations that go along with contributing to the gene pool, should dictate all decision-making.

Biology is a scientific excuse for l e t h a r g y that leads to DISGUST and MADNESS. It is also an instance of unoriginal thinking. No society has had complete control over its citizenry's sexuality, but every society, by whatever means necessary, has hampered its citizenry's sexuality. The society gets into our bloodstream by way of our biological agendas. So to find the orgasms that cannot be taken away from us, to embrace the orgasms that are entirely our own—that are celebrations of ourselves and are happening outside the auspicies of biology and its diabolically limiting view of our purpose on this earth—is to find further escape from the drastic amputations beset upon us by the society. This is why *the VICARIOUS ORGASM is the orgasm that results in REVOLUTION rather than a CIGARRETTE.*

Notice that these orgasms are produced by ourselves, for ourselves, and we are to be found at the beginning and the end of all of these orgasms. Notice that in these moments of self-ordaining orgasmic splendor our self-censorships do not survive. The mind thinks bigger and has much bigger ideas and goals than the body, and so, of course, the mind has much bigger orgasms than the body.

Procreation can happen in the worst conditions; to reach a state of higher love with someone is **the soul's** *TRUE ATHLETICISM.*

The Haughwout Building is also where **Elisha Otis** would first successfully enact his experiment and invention. Otis would be the first one to bring suspense into mechanization. His invention—an ongoing hanging—a belief in matter melted into disbelief, an elevation in increments, a technologically advanced stutter, was the *elevator.*

The elevator was first used in these cast-iron buildings of SoHo and is another reason that historians think of these buildings as precursors to the *skyscraper.* Another innovative attribute of these cast-iron buildings is the very large windows that increased ventilation for the factory's interior and brought sunlight to laborers who hadn't had much to do with sunlight before.

Sunlight is where we must take **our bodies** *recently transformed into* **gigantic** ***KISSES***, and if it is a cloudy day while you walk these streets, find the sunlight anyway in front of **515 Broadway**, where you will find an original **Bishop's crook lamp.** These are the original lampposts of SoHo. The entire ornament is a huge uncurling leaf illuminating itself. This is an example of Mother Nature finding surreptitious and ingenious ways to make her way back onto the island of her exile. The next time the wind blows, feel it caressing your skin. This wind is another example of ***Mother Nature disguising herself*** as a COSMOPOLITAN so she can be with us on the streets of SoHo.

At **550 Broadway** is a building from the 1850s. This was the original **Tiffany's** store. The building has been altered and is now in a slightly downtrodden state, but the aura of the place remains. Tiffany's moved from this location up to the formerly much more fasionable Union Square. Eventually, the store would end up on 57th Street and Fifth Avenue, where it is today.

The green statue of the masculine figure holding up a giant clock on his shoulders that adorns the front cornice of Tiffany's has adorned the façade of each Tiffany's location. The image of a man holding up a clock with all of his strength has within it a profound proclamation that a man's entire life is a concentrated effort to expand the duration of his erection physically and morally. A man's stamina is directly related to a woman's pleasure. The entire activity at the basis of Tiffany's infamy, the act of a man buying a diamond for a woman, is actually a desperate attempt to impress her with materials so that she will not rest in the primal, subconscious understanding that he is not pleasing her sexually.

On the southwest corner of Broadway and Spring Street, there is a **Chase Manhattan Bank** that has a few ATMs—automatic teller machines—in its foyer. The lines that form for these ATMs are often particularly intense because **these ATMs are located at what Sam Schulman calls SoHo's** ***nexus of spiritual beauty.***

When the line gets longer than the room that houses these ATMs, the line of people curls like a snake. In the story of Adam and Eve, the serpent represents impatience. As mentioned earlier, Kafka once wrote, *"IMPATIENCE is what got us kicked out of Paradise in the first place; lethargy is what keeps us from getting back in."* He concludes by saying that "impatience and lethargy are the same thing." (He must have been a double-decker-bus tour guide at some point in his career.)

Stand in the middle of this living landmark, this Chase Bank ATM line, whether or not you need cash. Feel the tortured patience of a long ATM line and note the extravagent wardrobes collaborating to create an art installation entitled "Snake Dance—the Exiled Children of Eve Waiting for Cash."

Just north of the Chase Bank, also on the west side of Broadway is the **Little Singer Building**, which was designed by one of the great and underrated New York architects, **Ernest Flagg.**

The Little Singer Building is a materialized exploration of

our masculine and feminine sides. *Tantra* **is the understanding that we are all composed of a masculine and *feminine* side who are cohabitants in our bodies and who are both GREAT LOVERS**. The vicarious orgasm, known to some as the covert public orgasm, is the consumation of the self-contained foreplay happening between our masculine and feminine sides all day.

The Little Singer Building's façade is a joyous co-existence and dance shared between green running cast-iron balconies and petite excursions of terra cotta. The two materials represent the masculine and feminine sides of our human existences finding a balance. Their ***flirtation* *results in DECORATION.***

Let us take our focused concentration from the lofty objectivity on the topic of our sexuality sent down by the Little Singer Building and concentrate this knowledge in an appreciation of another human being's beauty.

FIXATE YOUR *lust* ON A SPECIFIC PERSON ON THE SIDEWALKS. Find a personification of your ability to enjoy your body, somebody who imbues your second chakra with a sense of adventure. Remember the vicarious orgasm, also known as *concentration's orgasm*, is also our opportunity to excercise our **muscles of homoeroticism**. I believe we are born to lust polyphonously and continually—if lusting after people of your own gender is not something you do regularly, do it now.

My initial introduction to homoeroticism came when I realized I was using the silent sexual acknowledgement from my guy friends in high school to lift my afternoons into ecstatic opinions about myself and my place in the world.

Homoeroticism is the unaware love affair between same-gendered individual entropies who, we must remember, are actually beings of limitless light who are uncomfortable in this human body. Man, l i m i t l e s s , is currently in a continuous, frustrated state of trying to express his i n f i n i t y while ruthlessly boundaried.

The central question of masculinity in a man's life: "Is he laughing *at* his homoeroticism or is he laughing *with* his homoeroticism?" The **flaming heterosexual** is laughing *with* the unaware love affairs he has with other men while the fraternity brother is usually laughing *at* the love affairs he is unaware of with other men.

What we are unaware of has more influence over our actions than what we are aware of. Our days are directed less by the women or men we are kissing and more by the actions and reactions we are having to the men or women in our lives we are never quite kissing.

To embrace this truth is to be a true heterosexual.

To deny this truth is to be an impotent homosexual. **Most HETEROSEXUAL MEN" are** IMPOTENT HOMO-EXUALS.

A "homophobe" is actually a man who has been driven inane by this truth.

This is why **Jean Genet's** play *The Maids* is one of the great exhibitions of masculinity in Western art. Genet called ejaculation "a little death" and was infuriated when he was released from prison because it was the only place where he could get laid consistently. In his play, twelve-year-old boys are dressed up in drag as maidservants and are at play in a drastic foreplay that results in their orgasmic death. This is what male heterosexuality looks like in its purest form.

Take yourself and your panting into **Dean and Deluca**, the posh gourmet food store on the corner of **Prince Street and Broadway**. The whole store is protected by the benevolent gods of decadence and the Dionysian love of food and wine. In my life, wherever materialism has died and become drab for me, Dionysus has triumphantly risen.

It is important to have a direct experience of tasting people along the aisles of Dean and Deluca. Some need more salt, some need a dab of hollandaise, some a sprinkle of paprika, but ***ALL NEED SOMETHING.***

Across the street you will find the **Guggenheim Museum of SoHo** which is a great exhibition hall and gift shop for standing near exciting, erotic humanity.

One time I was in the Guggenheim SoHo during an exhibition of the Russian painter **Wassily Kandinsky's** drawings, and the breathing and the women were so beautiful around me that I became capable of doing what Kandinsky always insisted was his essential talent, which was *hearing* color. I was vicariously coming and hearing the colors of Kandinsky's drawings, even though most of the drawings were done with charcoal and were black-and-white. To think some people called that "Tuesday afternoon."

All you men who have to work arduously to discover your multi-orgasmic abilities, should send your life energy, your breath, into your scrotums and squeeze right now. Try to compress your breath into your scrotum and hold it there for a full minute. Women who, when fully appreciating themselves, are mutli-orgasmic standing still, should right now caress your entire body softly with your imagination.

The tantric energy of any person is happening no matter how oblivious he or she is to it; however, the energy they give off seems to increase with their awareness of it. *Try looking at paintings while standing next to marvelous moments that have become human bodies.*

Whenever you choose to get back to **Spring Street**, take a right. As we move westward on Spring Street, fixate on passersby and try to match their breathing; establish as much eye contact as they will allow.

As we cross over **Mercer Street** stand on the cobblestones that cover the street. **GET IN TOUCH WITH THE COBBLESTONES' TEMPERATURE.** How does it feel against your skin? Feel the energy from the antique cobblestones rise up through the soles of your feet and then up your spinal cord—your life nerve.

In the distance, to the right, is a sudden, astonishing view of the **Chrysler Building**. See and then feel its erection to the north. Let it inspire you. (**For more about the Chrysler Building, refer to "The Midtown Rush Hour Tour."**)

Next we approach **Greene Street.** Along the east side of Greene Street, from here to Canal Street, is the longest consecutive stretch of cast-iron façades in the world. Allow every meticulous pilaster, every Ionic column, all the pediments and the entire entablature of this day, these visions, to wash over you. Continue your testicular or vaginal breathing. Your mind is now participating in sex just as much as your sex organs and you are making love to these buildings.

*This state of **building-to-orgasm** is your true state. **The people we are when we are on the brink of an orgasm is who we really are.***

There is nothing vicarious about this orgasm for you. This is the orgasm you are having for yourself, by yourself, about yourself, all over yourself, and the entire world is reduced to a voyeur.

You are your own greatest lover!

If you can still walk, move farther across Spring Street over to **Wooster Street.** Turn up, up, up and move north on Wooster Street. There are sexy, sardonic, aloof boutiques all around you.

Here we can take a moment to recognize that the second chakra is a limited apparatus and that the vicarious orgasm is only using it as a launch pad into the higher chakras.

Our lower chakras are the ones that view SoHo as a place to be seen.

All around us on Wooster Street, the second chakra and the organs and thought patterns of pleasure are announcing themselves through lycra, spandex, cotton, arrogance, wide-brimmed hats, purses, leers, fine-tuned assemblages of flesh upon flesh, shiny colors, credit cards, and silk.

As we move north along Wooster Street, I am announcing to you that I am a huge fan of pleasure and I digress regularly into evenings of wanton perspiring and nude massages. And yet, I recognize, even here on sexy, pleasurable Wooster Street, the esteemed difference and wide chasm that seperates pleasure and joy.

The second chakra knows nothing of joy. *It knows how to* PARTY and when it comes to physicalized orgasms, it is a vortex and a landmark for all time. However, timeless bliss is the product of collaborations between our existences in the abstract and the concrete. Joy has no opposite and, in fact, it is the lessons of our lives calling out to us, "Your confusion is sexy!"

The opposite of pleasure is pain. They are both experiences to be experienced, but so many burn up in the futile attempts to have one without the other.

At **141 Wooster Street**, between Prince and Houston streets, buzz the buzzer to the **Dia Art Center** on the second floor. The buzzer is labeled the **Earth Room.** The Earth Room is a permanent installation that rests upstairs.

As we prepare to enter the environs of the Earth Room, I would like to personally thank the human body for its genius and recognize it as a great collaborator in our ongoing spiritual awakening.

This tour has become a love poem to the human body, my favorite version of inifinity. Style is the pursuit of our body's infinity, and SoHo certainly is stylish.

Enter the **Earth Room:** this is the most ***outside*** you have been all day. You have just walked inside to get outside. The room itself is very SoHo. It has pristine white walls that are gently anesthetic—and it is snotty, perfectly.

This is the greatest use of valuable New York real estate currently exisiting on the island of Manhattan.

The Earth Room's power is in its effortless beauty, especially when compared to the ecosystem of Wooster Street, which is trying so hard to make an impression on us. The Earth Room reminds us that SoHo is provisional. From the Earth's perspective, SoHo is a snowflake in a sandstorm.

From the other side of the Earth Room, you can see nature rushing toward us.

Nature has come to greet us. Her legs are spread-eagled, and she is panting.

I just came.

Strolling through SoHo is actually a safari through a sweating erogenous zone. SoHo is not a district or a neighborhood; it is living sex. Everything within it, the stores, the historic landmarks, its stories, the pedestrians, everything results in sex. This is where the city, sexier than any of us could ever imagine, is teaching us that we are scoring all day long. Our sexual frustrations are actually fantasies promoted and are now one step closer to **actualization.**

A Tour of the Empire State Building Observation Deck Line

At first you doubted me but then—I rose!
—Dr. Frederick Baker

(Read this material while standing, physically or metaphorically, in line for the Empire State Building's observation deck—**34th Street and Fifth Avenue.** Tickets are sold for the observation deck in the basement of the Empire State Building. The observation deck is open until midnight.)

(It is recommended that you be a part of the longest lines possible. Aim for noon on summer days or any holiday evening.)

Merely a totem pole, the **Empire State Building's** essential purpose is to be danced around. A totem pole is an ornament and a centralizing gesture created by a tribe to bring its people together. *The tribe who built this totem pole is the human race.* Therefore, the tribal ceremony happening on top of it is comprised of international souls and this is happening in the middle of a metropolis that belongs to the world more than any other place.

The true landmark here is not the totem pole, but the *line of people* lining up each day in and around and on top of the enormous totem pole.

The **observation deck line** is a sacred ceremony of internationality waiting to get high. As we ascend eight hundred feet into the air, we all have different ways of feeling the upliftment.

To make the journey to the **eighty-sixth floor** with a bunch of uninspired, spoiled brats followed by a trip with the truly curious is to have clear proof that altitude is a state of mind. Certain women have taken me to much more incredible heights than the Empire State Building ever has.

THE OBSERVATION DECK LINE: an international congregation of souls convening to GET HIGH.

The first bank of elevators we will get into will ascend to the eightieth floor. The apartments of the Empire State Building reside between the eightieth and eighty-fifth floors. We will be taking the private elevators that operate exclusively between these floors to rise up to the observation deck on the **eighty-sixth floor**. The entire building around us was made possible because of this innovative shift system of elevators developed by the **Otis Company.** By assigning different altitudes to different elevators, a relay race is created between them, and their proliferation throughout accelerates service to such a degree that it becomes practical to build a hundred floors of rentable office space.

Together, let us get in line. We probably have anywhere from half an hour to an hour and a half to stand here together and **resist our need to *anticipate*** the observation deck of the Empire State Building.

Feel the electricity of all the original spirits around us. *Notice all the different* FACIAL EXPRESSIONS *as they* HAPPEN. This is some of the greatest theater you and I will ever see.

Feel the effluvious, silent scream of pain emanating from all those who are in this line but cannot stand the agony of waiting. They are not really waiting to get to the top of the Empire State Building, they are waiting for Vesuvius to stop smoking.

When the Empire State Building was first completed it was innovative and intimidating, not only because of its altitude but also for the speed with which it was completed.

The building is an exhilarated American landmark, which is to say, anything that is beautiful about it is accidental. THIS IS THE CLIMAX OF CASS GILBERT'S DESCRIPTION OF A SKYSCRAPER AS "A MACHINE THAT MAKES THE LAND PAY."

William Lamb, the architect of the building, viewed himself as a living extension of the entrepreneur's will. Thus the very design of the building was governed by profitability. The goal was to build the Empire State Building as quickly, as economically, and as cheaply as possible and hope that the renters and the observation deck would make the whole enterprise profitable.

Lamb, an unwitting apostle of the city-teacher, was only partially aware that the Empire State Building was only built for the purpose of creating the observation deck line and ritual. Notice that merely half a century later Lamb and his own selfish intentions are interred with his bones and yet his service to the city has survived him.

The first hole was dug for the building's foundation—the shovel hits the ground for that initial hole—seven days after the stock market crashed in 1929.

Lamb's description of the Empire State Building's construction as **"THOUGHTLESS" was his way of saying "IDEAL."** The Empire State Building was completed in thirteen months.

Workers constructed, on average, a floor a day and during one ten-day stretch, fourteen floors. The whole project was finished five million dollars under budget.

The Empire State Building is the central cathedral of this city's skyline. It is equated with Cologne's Cathedral, the Duomo in Florence, and the pyramids of Egypt and Chichén Itzá as a great structure that is also a mascot and/or symbol of what the city stands for. Unlike those great cathedrals, the Empire State Building did not take hundreds of years to build; it took thirteen months. Unlike those esteemed European cathedrals, the Empire State Building did not take several generations of sacrifice to be actualized. The population watched it being built with the detached perspective of spectators; the main purpose for *this* central cathedral was not to reveal or revel in reverence but rather in our know-how.

Speed is one of the major themes and ingredients of the twentieth century. Some of us have gone mad with speed, accelerated into lives that have become impersonations of a highway. ***SPEED HAS PROVEN TO US, UNCONSCIOUSLY, THAT NO MATTER HOW FAST WE GO WE ARE STILL NOT ESCAPING OURSELVES.*** Once we realized this catastrophe, the twentieth century followed logically. (**Also, refer to Speed Levitch's life.**)

Therefore, the Empire State Building—as an homage to speed, technology, and efficiency—is also an homage to metamorphisized hysteria.

*

NEW YORK CITY: a GIANT human being getting caught up in a GIANT trip.

*

As we continue moving along with the line, step by step, feel the notion of stranger melt away as we share in this moment of waiting. There are no strangers here, there are the other dancers who, along with us, are forming ***a ceremony and a gathering that we call—for the sake of convenience—a line.***

Take a moment to observe the different reactions to the **wait** going on around you. Watch the alterations of people's spirits as we get nearer and nearer the first bank of elevators. With each step, you are closer than you have ever been before.

"Anticipation kills," **Jean Klein** once said. "Every time we fall out of the moment it is a catastrophe," **Huang Po** taught. It would seem that **anticipation is one of the most monstrously conceived anti-*Cruise* conspiracies that we face. It is the busiest expressway from the moment**

Another characteristic that the Duomo, the Cologne Cathedral, the Empire State Building, and the pyramids all have in common is that each one attempts to explain mankind to the universe.

The Empire State Building is a modern pyramid in discourse with the ancient pyramids of Chichén Itzá and Egypt. It is not a pyramid built to house any specific pharaoh, and it is not built in reverence to any specific God. It is a secular pyramid built in the name of *masculinity.*

Masculinity is neediness attempting to prove that it is has everything it needs. It is mankind's ongoing, deluded need to explain himself to the universe. This is a necessarily desperate situation because **there is NO explanation and the universe couldn't care LESS.**

The Empire State Building is impressive without being opulent. It is huge and humble, the same combination of characteristics that make a man *debonair.* It is effective, strong, durable, and its despair is impossible to discern. There is a series of illuminated panels on one wall of the lobby where this building portrays itself as the eighth wonder of the world. We will never know if this is empty boastfulness or true confidence. Note that

I **HAVE JUST DESCRIBED THE EMPIRE STATE BUILDING AND A SUCCESSFUL FRATERNITY BROTHER, SIMULTANEOUSLY.**

When **F. Scott Fitzgerald** first stood atop the **Empire State Building** he said he was "disillusioned and crushed to see clearly from this view that New York City, indeed, is *not* limitless," as he had always assumed it was. This was the day F. Scott Fitzgerald officially became a lost alcoholic.

Wasn't Fitzgerald's reaction to the this view the same reaction **Alexander the Great** has in that famous moment right after he has just conquered the last district of the known world, when he weeps because he realizes there are no more worlds left to conquer?

In this moment, Alexander is truly great. He is standing alone at the end of the world, facing all of his failed attempts to explain himself.

When **Alexander The Great** saw the view, *he wept*, for there were no more worlds to conquer . . .

We are surrounded by modern technology and archaic stone. We are standing inside a series of extractions from an Indiana rockbed, inside a congregation of rocks; we are standing in a certain kind of cave. But what good is it all without love and togetherness?

When we get to the eightieth floor there will be another line that will snake through abandoned offices on our way to another bank of elevators. As we traverse this line, we will pass by windows that bestow upon us our first altitudinous view of the skyline. The mountainous **30 Rockefeller Center** is facing us with its soft yet hard granite look and the large sign that says "GE." **(For more about 30 Rock, refer to "The Midtown Rush Hour Tour.")**

The architectural definition of skyscraper is a structure that is actually a skeleton of steel with different materials hanging off the steel skeleton. The materials could be granite, fiberglass, or tissue paper—the actual skyscraper is the steel skeleton, shooting up into the sky. Throughout earlier architectural history, to build tall buildings one needed large, masonry walls at the base to support the structure. With the invention called skyscraper a tall building can be built without excess supports that take up space, and every inch, from the bottom to the top of the structure, is rentable.

My definition of skyscraper is a little more metaphysical than the architects' and, I might add, a lot more fun. I would say that **a skyscraper is any structure that *DEFIES* the imaginings of the people of its time.** And so, according to my definition, the **Brooklyn Bridge** is a skyscraper, the **Flatiron Building** is a skyscraper, the **entire skyline of Chicago** is a skyscraper, the **early Roman aqueducts** were all skyscrapers, the **Tower of Babel** was a skyscraper, and perhaps the first skyscraper of biblical history was the **burning bush**—that strange, blazing botany so confident that the human race prefers liberation. (I've had my doubts.)

Even more historically accurate in our hearts and in our guts, however, is the skyscraper formed every time two beings share each other's mystery, and gaze upon each other's entablature nudity. A new lover is a skyscraper.

Many major Midtown Manhattan landmarks were constructed in the time we refer to as the **Depression**. Each skyscraper was an economic and emotional attempt to excite ourselves, and each skyscraper erected during that time was an attempt to wake us up out of our depression. **The Empire State Building is also a sculpture entitled "*PLEASE DON'T BE DEPRESSED*."** It is an enormous gesture of pointing up toward the bright side of life.

As we get off the elevator and enter the Empire State Building's observation deck, recognize that this moment will never happen again. Consider all the infinite paths, incredible and bewildering, drunken, stumbling anecdotes that have happened throughout the last 15,000 years of neurotic disequilibrium that has created every single being in this room right now and that has brought us all here.

This is a summoning. ***We have all been brought here to see this tumultuous view for reasons we may never know.***

The Midtown Rush Hour Tour

New York City is a magnificent catastrophe.
—Le Corbusier

The illusion that we are separate from one another is an optical delusion of our consciousness.
—Albert Einstein

We are *evolving* despite ourselves and nowhere is this truth more clear than during rush hour—the dance of quiet desperation.

Walt Whitman in "Crossing Brooklyn Ferry" mentions "The quick, abrupt questions that rise from within." It is these very questions that move rush hour to rush and it is the answers to these questions that cause the buses and trains to accelerate.

Our process—a mess—nonetheless, is one of acquiring the fine-tuned taste for living; that special Szechuan delight of flavored progress that makes one a lover of the world rather than an enemy of it.

E. M. Cioran said, "The only ones who are not murderers are the bon vivants."

Evolution is, for humans, an inward motion. Improvements to the human race incited by Mother Nature's dynamic, rock 'n' roll lifestyle are no longer happening to the human body but to the human psyche.

What's really evolving **in us these days is our talent for *living*.**

The process of ourselves becoming even more ourselves is the most outrageous, most challenging Olympic event of all time.

Midtown Manhattan's rush hour is one of the greatest places to view this incredible athleticism—the human race fighting and dying for yards on the battlefield of bliss.

Everything we could ever be is crying down to us from the crests of skyscrapers and green running hillsides, "Let's ride! Let's roll!"

People pursuing success and opportunity are truly pursuing visions of themselves as happier people, whether they even know what happiness is or not. The city, a great magician here to aid even the most inadvertent pursuits of enlightenment, has constructed Midtown Manhattan so that **the human beings dwelling here will eventually realize that THEY ARE TALLER than skyscrapers.**

Midtown Manhattan is proof that there are no strangers. The interconnectedness of the human race is happening every time we agree that green means go, that smoking in hotel lobbies is wrong, and that five o' clock is a good time to go home. Midtown is the final proof that cities are not really the practical manifestation of commerce. *Cities are the manifestation of our need for each other.*

Midtown is an exhibition, unaware that it is exhibiting anything. People rally for and against political causes on the streets of the city and are often very successful in creating a public scene. Yet they lose sight of the performance. The result, of course, is bad theater.

Midtown is filled with street performers and each one of them believes his or her participation is more important than anybody else's.

Midtown also demonstrates that another major reason for a city to form is for the ease of eavesdropping. During the average weekday, Midtown is one of the greatest places the world has ever known for the possibility of listening in on the lives of others without having to actually deal with them.

Right now, Midtown is an art installation and shared improvisation. The "average" afternoon in Midtown Manhattan is a masterpiece co-created by everyone involving themselves with everyone else involved.

And if compassion is the understanding that ***WE'RE ALL IN THIS TOGETHER,*** that we don't exist autonomously, that each of us is a celebration contributing to a larger celebration, then the more we exercise active compassion the greater our ability to enjoy each other's participations in each other's lives.

Life is the art of crafting moments. Our moments sculpted out of time and space and each other are always to be found in an eternal art gallery at the end of each day. **The art gallery that houses all of our retrospectives is the u n i v e r s e .**

The goal of this tour is to become enlightened.

Welcome to Midtown Manhattan!

WE BEGIN AT THE INFORMATION BOOTH IN GRAND CENTRAL TERMINAL— 42ND STREET AND PARK AVENUE:

(A cruise of Grand Central is recommended during the rush hour, which is 7 AM to 9 AM and 4 PM to 6 PM on weekdays, or on any major holiday.)

We are standing in the middle of **Grand Central Terminal.** Which is to say, we are standing in the original "Gateway to the New World" and one of the great rooms of North America. Grand Central Terminal is the building that became a vortex and created the twentieth-century explosion known as Midtown Manhattan.

And what is the twentieth century? Is it the most perfect Marx Brothers film ever made? **Perhaps it is the time when nature, which has come for the umpteenth time to greet us, finally says, "YOU'RE STEPPING ON MY TOE!"** Is the twentieth century a certain shaman's journey honoring the ancestors? Is it a panty raid in a distant, far-more-evolved galaxy?

Standing here at the **information booth** in Grand Central Terminal, ***we are surrounded by the interconnectedness of the human race, the silent togetherness of the alienated.*** This is the dance of the large, lonely crowds scattering around this room. Watch as these individuals, the movie stars and divas of their own self-centered dramas, move about you. No matter how they portray themsleves, no matter how they act toward each other, they are all sharing this room and they are all contributing equally to the formation of a sculpture entitled

"Grand Central Terminal Main Concourse—at This Moment in Eternity."

The enormous, vaulted, aquamarine ceiling is the sky with all the constellations one sees in the night sky. It is an enormous astrological chart designed backward so that we can see the cosmos from the point of view of the gods.

Time and space are having *a lover's spat all around you.* They are using the eighty-thousand-square-foot Tennessee marble floor and a hundred-and-fifty-foot vaulted ceiling to stage their argument.

Walk around the main concourse, note the original chandeliers that hang from the ceiling like enormous earrings. The seventy-five-foot-tall windows accomodate five bridges that pedestrians use to move across the width of the building high above the crowds below. ***The windows become opera balconies during rush hour, providing an exceptional view of the vast movement of people and time.*** See if the anti-Cruise will stop you in your attempt to get up into those windows.

The anti-Cruise has been consistently censorious toward those of us interested in appreciating the beauty of this place. There is even a law on the books that restricts kissing on the floor of the main concourse of Grand Central. Officially, the law is a prohibition against any activities that block the moving pedestrian traffic in this busy place. In reality, this law is the action of those who are afraid of human possibility.

Walk among the living, moving daily landmark called **rush hour.**

Rush hour is an army mobilizing on a city every morning and retreating every afternoon. ***RUSH HOUR is a collectivity of beings becoming a single being that prioritizes its life according to comfort and is only interested in the destinations we can run toward,*** *ignoring the destinations that come for us.*

The commuter who misses his train is in limbo during that ephemeral interval between the train he missed and the next train. When those fifteen minutes he spends waiting for the next train become the greatest fifteen minutes of his life, he's cruising. This limbo period of self between trains is the final exam in a course called "**Appreciating *Beauty* in the *Unexpected*.**"

Grand Central Terminal is an ongoing exam that asks questions like, "Do we have the stamina to laugh at the world among the exhaust smoke of a train we just missed?"

The **feeling of arrival**, that feeling of being grand and central simultaneously, is the sensation of an adventure coming just as you, in turn, become the adventure's discovery. When you stand still amid the interconnectedness of all things, the chaos is genuine and clearly visible and you become more senstive to the adventures that are constantly coming for us. **GRAND CENTRAL IS GRAND AND IT IS CENTRAL BECAUSE IT POSSESSES THE AURA OF CONSTANT ARRIVAL. A GIGANTIC SENSE OF ARRIVING IS THAT BEAUTIFUL SENSATION THAT YOU ARE STANDING EXACTLY WHERE YOU'RE SUPPOSED TO BE—COSMICALLY ON SCHEDULE.**

This fully experienced arrival is the essential ingredient of an orgasm, too. An orgasm feels so good because it is a moment when you are sure there is no place else you'd rather be and there is nothing else you should be doing and there is no feeling you'd rather be feeling. (**Also, refer to "A Tour of Soho, or How to Render Sexual Frustration Obsolete."**)

Find one of the wide sweeping ramps swirling in and around this room and walk up and down it. The entire design of Grand Central is based on the same thought that caused Caesar to make the downward sloping hills around Rome steeper. This made the hills easier for Roman legions to descend and, therefore, accelerated their pace. Those same hills became more treacherous and more acutely uphill for the armies marching toward Rome.

FORTY-SECOND STREET RUSH HOUR: What surrounds you right now is all illusion; ***an illusion we are here to fully participate in.***

The ramps are excellent places to serenade the commuters madly committing themselves to locomotion. Take a moment to sing out love poems to all this to and fro.

Once we are on the **lower level**, walk this recapitulation of the main concourse until you are facing the famous **Oyster Bar.** In front of the front doors is a set of four arches facing each other, forming four corners. When you whisper into one of the corners, your voice is amplified in the corner that stands diagonally from wherever you are. Go to these arches and have one of the truly important conversations of your life.

Right before the actual front doors of the restaurant is a large window. Looking through it, one has a sweeping vista view of the elongated counter of the Oyster Bar. ***How do you think Degas would have handled this scene?***

Enjoy the safari journey back upstairs, and once there, walk through the **entrance hall**, complete with its original chandeliers from 1913. An intrinsic lime-green color runs subtly around the walls and window frames. This is an eccentric green that the renovators of this building meticulously researched and examined so that they could re-create the specific green color used by the original architects. The green is light, feminine. It is the embroidered, back-lit springlike effervescence of our collective arrival into this room, into this city, into this world.

Walk outside of Grand Central Terminal's front door.

We have arrived. We now stand on **42nd Street**. At first, 42nd Street might be overwhelming because it is so frenetic and so huge. Take a deep breath and remind yourself that what surrounds you right now is an illusion. ***This is an illusion we have arrived in and we are here to fully participate in it.*** Also remember that when you feel lost in Midtown Manhattan you are just being precise about your true position in the universe.

Perhaps rush hour is a living relay race that cannot be won or lost, a race daring us to stop running. Let's stand still for several moments here amid the completely energized and desperate action-thriller that surrounds us. Watch the adventure unwinding around you. If someone bumps into you, allow your body to go with the flow. The people bumping into you are only working you into the dance.

The flow of people flowing for the sake of flow around you is in pursuit of illusions. For the most part, they are caught on a loop of their brain's design, and so they will appear to be rushed. Impatience is the brain's strategy.

The ceaseless flow of pedestrians echoes the ceaseless flow of truth, for truth is a flow flowing for the sake of the flow. This is also true of our saliva. Our saliva keeps flowing even when we stop.

Examine with tender, savory, meticulous attention
the façade of the CHANIN BUILDING:
fish are swimming across the aquarium called 42nd Street.

Directly in front of Grand Central Terminal, is **Park Avenue South**, a name invented by real estate brokers. The road was originally called Fourth Avenue. Their motivation for changing the name of the road was to make it more expensive by associating it with ritzy Park Avenue.

The green bridge that straddles 42nd Street is part of the ingenious series of bridges and ramps that wrap around Grand

Central's body like a corset or a pair of lover's arms. It is a pair of lover's arms when the traffic is flowing evenly. It is a corset when there is congestion.

These ramps allow vehicular traffic to flow uninterrupted along the trajectory of Park Avenue, even though Grand Central sits right in the middle of the street, **THE BOLDEST INTERRUPTION.**

To the far right is **Madison Avenue**. If you look at the original maps of Midtown Manhattan, you will see that Madison Avenue is not on them. Madison Avenue began as a service road for **Fifth Avenue**. Fifth Avenue was, at that time, "Millionaire's Row," a long series of aristocratic mansions. Madison Avenue was a dirt road lined with gardener's shacks and horse sheds, and was not to become a proper road until the automobile made its appearance on the island.

For three hundred of the first four hundred supposed years of New York City's supposed existence Midtown Manhattan does not exist.

Will you look at Madison Avenue today! May I restate, recapitulate, and generally regurgitate . . . when you are standing in **Midtown Manhattan**, you are standing in the middle of a **twentieth-century invention!** A city that grew up at the rate of an explosion, spurred by a never-ending cultural explosion! A series of test tubes whirling, gurgling, boiling, a radioactive atom swirling! In certain exclusive circles this Midtown Manhattan is known as *"Unhappiness Learning How to Be HAPPY!"* and/or it is referred to as, "A Giant Feeling of Need Imploding!" and also "A Secret Return to the Original Deities."

I call Midtown Manhattan "The Reasons Natasha-Hiding-from-Simone Suddenly Turns to Me and Says, 'I Love You, but I'm Repressing This Love Because I Have Societal Responsibilities, and I Have to Be a Good Citizen from Now On!' "

This is ludicrousness and this cannot last! Midtown Manhattan will eventually sink and retake its rightful mythological title—Atlantis.

Midtown Manhattan is the twentieth-century TANTRUM in a moment of self-awareness.

Bring yourself to the 42nd Street and Park Avenue consciousness and turn left on 42nd Street. You will see yourself involved in a gigantic mirror reflection that is the exterior of a building. This is one of the original four hotels that New York Central Railroad built around Grand Central Terminal. This one, the Commodore, is now the renovated **Hyatt Regency Hotel**. Its interior is an example of **MODERNITY dimming the lights,** taking off its clothes, and seducing us.

Across the street from the revolving door entrances of the Hyatt is the **Chanin Building**. This building was designed by **Irwin Chanin**, one of the great architects of New York City and simultaneously one of its great theatrical producers: he builds theaters on the top floors of all of his buildings. Chanin built stage-set skyscrapers, constantly adding to the most enormous theater piece on earth. He is a nondualist taking action. He is conscious of the fact that *HE MAKES LOVE TO THE WORLD BY ADORNING IT WITH PLATFORMS.*

Note the wild botany engraved throughout the main cornice line above the Chanin Building's front entrance. This is a photosynthesis of stone happening right before us. These are plants that have overcome their need for sunlight and are blossoming on their own—a special manifestation labeled "psychadelic" by ethobotanists.

The leaves of the Chanin Building have a life of their own, and yet blend in so well with the cityscape, *it makes one wonder if all of Midtown Manhattan is just the ACID TRIP **Aldous Huxley** wanted to have,* the longed-for trip of the man who reminded humans that they are totally useless, and possibly dangerous, without self-awareness.

Even from this 42nd Street and Lexington Avenue consciousness one can see clearly that the situation happening around us is filled with unspeakable torment. There is so much totally unnoticed interconnectedness happening on this intersection. **The gigantic human understandings displaying themselves in the enormous series of complementary movements between the cars and pedestrians in front of us are the same gigantic understandings that will one day make us telepathic, group-conscious beings.**

Eventually we not only will be able to silently agree about the direction of traffic; we will be experiencing anger, love, and lust unanimously.

When Midtown Manhattan becomes an enlightened home instead of a bad imitation of ancient Rome, we will be standing in this intense field of vibration that we call, for the sake of convenience, 42nd Street, and will be able to hear everyone who has ever used the phrase "that's funny" to replace laughter, actually laugh.

Across from the Chanin Building, is the **Chrysler Building,** designed in 1929 by **William Van Alen**, who as a young architect dropped out of the French École des Beaux-Arts because he was bored.

*

Zeus, the manufacturer of all lightning, refers to Midtown rush hour as a "direct hit!"

*

The Chrysler Building is the semblance of a budding flower and a spaceship preparing for launch. Watch how it flares outward, exploding with terraces at several decisive tiers, accompanied by expressionistic images of automobiles driving up the building as if it were a divine highway to the unknown.

The rondels in the façade are ENORMOUS CHRYSLER RADIATOR CAPS. Abstract engravings of automobiles wrap around corners of the building, looking as if the trunks of the cars were pursuing the hoods. The eagles depicted by the building's traditional gargoyles are gargantuan reproductions of the 1928 Chrysler's hood ornament. *The BLAZING PYRAMID atop the Chrysler Building is a replica of the FRONT GRILLE of a 1928 CHRYSLER.*

Walter Chrysler, the businessman-entrepeneuer-pharaoh building a large ornament to commemmorate his name and memory, insisted that the building be the tallest in the world upon completion. New York City inspired many entrepreneurial men of this era to fight for altitude. Their sexual fantasies were making these decisions in collusion with their practicality. In New York terminology this is known as real estate speculation.

While the Chrysler Building was being built, a rival for the title of the tallest man-made structure in the world was under construction—**40 Wall Street**. **(Refer, also, to "Wall Street: The Story of What Happened to Our Intimacy.")** When the Chrysler Building looked like it had reached its maximum height, the architects of 40 Wall Street added an extra two feet to their structure, believing that the addition would make their building the tallest in the world.

Van Alen, however, heeding the calls of the Gods of Masculinity, had been constructing the now famous pyramid of the Chrysler Building within the fuselage of the building itself, hiding it from the outside world. When the pyramid was completed, Van Alen had the laborers ceremoniously raise it out of the building and fasten it to the top, the addition adding 123 feet to the Chrysler Building and making it the tallest building in the world. Mr. Chrysler was now a pharaoh with the tallest pyramid of all. **Walter Chrysler and his erection could be seen all over town.**

Mr. Chrysler and his building would experience one of architectural history's greatest emasculations, however, with the completion of the Empire State Building only eleven months later. **If architecture is the history of all phallic emotion, the CHRYSLER BUILDING has grown to become a cathedral to castration.**

I have often wept at the base of this cosmic disappointment.

Castration is when someone is trying to "save you from disappointment" when there is no disappointment in the room. Castration is when someone gives you advice that leaves you feeling stupid. **Castration is someone's sudden moment of insecurity hunting down anything that moves.** Castration is happening whenever you are excited but—for fear of exhibiting it in public—you act cool. Castration is the ongoing, invisible desecration of our spirits by means of contradicting us for the sake of competion. ***Those who are truly mad with rage in this world are everywhere, and wherever they are, they need contradiction to keep them from killing us all.***

A recurring dream I have had in my dream life has been an earthquake dream in which I am standing in the shadow of the Chrysler Building. In the middle of the violent earthquake, the top of the Chrysler Building falls. Plunging down the enormous length of the building, the point lands directly in my hand. The next day the entire city is decimated and there are pyres being set up on street corners to burn all the dead bodies strewn about. But I am ecstatic to have the tip of the Chrysler Building's antenna in my pocket. I then come upon a half-shattered storefront window and there is a large handwritten sign hanging there that reads, WILL PAY $9,000 FOR THE TIP OF THE CHRYLER BUILDING. I am standing there in a state of great confusion. Should I hold on to the greatest souvenir of my life or sell it for $9,000?

Fade to BLACK.

The walls of the **Chrysler Building's lobby** are covered with wild marble that swirls with dizzy excitation. If this marble could speak it would remind us, "It don't mean a thing if it ain't got that swing."

The lobby of the Chrysler Building is a centralized cathedral, complete with dim, religious lighting.

The question arises: If this is a church, where is she/he/it and what is she/he/it like?

The lobby—a central cathedral—drives energy and focus toward its altar. Clearly, the altar is the security guard's desk placed as it is at the top and middle of the lobby's centrality.

The priests of this church are the security guards. The religion being practiced here is security.

The elevators in the **Chrysler Building** are covered with designs found during the archaeological discovery of King Tut's tomb, which was being unearthed as the Chrysler Building was being constructed. Look inside the **elevators–They are tombs** that ASCEND and descend . . .

The elevator doors are covered with designs derived from the archaeological discovery of **King Tut's tomb**, which was unearthed around the same time that the Chrsyler Building was on the drawing board. **(Also, refer to "A Tour of the Empire State Building Observation Deck Line.")**

Look inside the elevators: they are moving tombs that ascend and descend.

The ceiling mural of the Chrysler Building's lobby is remarkable. It is a vast homage to labor and transportation. Here man experiences perspiration perspired for reasons beyond bodily function. To believe the process of sweating is a manifestation of "good works" is to believe that *to do* is the bridge between ourselves and feelings of transcendence. **Jean Klein** once said, "The human race is not made up of human beings. Mostly they are human doings."

During any sojourn through Midtown Manhattan one will encounter a simmering celebration of doing. The whole place is busy, announcing to the world, "There are things you can DO to become somebody!"

Stand for a moment under the sprawling mural above you and imagine yourself **free from doership.** Just be. *Imagine yourself free from the need to DO anything.* Stand still and become everything you've ever wanted to be. **(For more about salvation, see "A Tour of the Cathedral of St. John The Divine: Cathedral Party.")**

From the center of the Chrysler Building's lobby take a left, and walk out the **Lexington Avenue exit**, past the lightning-bolt staircase that ascends into a black cosmos.

Once standing outside the door on **Lexington Avenue** itself, take a right up Lexington Avenue. We are now heading toward another art deco building in the distance: the indomitable **General Electric Building.**

"Art deco" refers to that form of architectural artistry that evolved during the artist's first contact with electricity and the energy of the modern age. It is an intense focus on instantaneousness and on the melting down of conventionality—that meek, agreed-upon filtering of reality.

To melt down conventionality is to deconstruct the images of convention, something all the major artistic movements of the twentieth century have in common. Movements as diverse as cubism, abstract expressionism, and pop art all find themselves distilling the superficial reality dictated to our physical senses into an expression of the physical senses that moves beyond the limitations of reality. **Matter is a curiosity exam.**

The top of the GE Building seems to be permanently struck

by lightning, forever energized by man's endeavors. The façade is **an** ongoing **contest** between ***man's energy*** and NATURE'S POWER.

Across the street, the beaux arts building is the post office called Grand Central Station. Today, this beaux arts building has a postmodern skyscraper sitting on top of it. The older architecture and the newer architecture are absorbed in an argument that is a building. They are connected for reasons they cannot understand. They are lovers.

Take a left on 44th Street and walk toward the enormous **Pan Am Building** that is now the **Met Life Building.**

Upon completion in 1963, the Pan Am Building was considered to be the largest office building ever built. Its arrogant stance in the middle of Park Avenue was deemed ruinous to Park Avenue's skyline.

The Met Life Building is a great addition to the New York City skyline because it is noticeable.

When I visited the Acropolis in Athens, I didn't notice people greatly agitated nor did I see great throngs thinking immensely or even shiftlessly. No one had a problem with the Parthenon. It sat in its famous way, and photographs were taken with a hypnotic rhythm. I have seen the Met Life Building stir radicals, melancholy lackadaisicals, happy-go-lucky frauds, and real estate agents. I have heard the cry and I have witnessed noble frustration.

This beleaguered experiment called civilization depends on lethargy. *Therefore, ENERGY and the ENERGIZING of each other is the GREATEST REVOLUTIONARY ACT.*

Facing the Met Life Building is the ornate **Helmsley Building.** This building was built by and for the company that built all of this splendor around us. It was called the **New York Central Railroad Company Building.**

There are two tunnels running through the Helmsley Building. As we walk through either one of them, we are passing under the patinated bridges of the 1903 ramp system.

As we walk under the Helmsley Building we are viewing a vast roadway, growing vaster. We are walking along the outskirts of a person's thoughts. In front of you is **Park Avenue**.

The person in question was **William Wilgus** and the place, **Fourth Avenue.** Originally this was a place of soot and screeching and huge machinery, and no one hung out there. Fourth Avenue still exists and is right in front of us, buried beneath our feet. Wilgus's thought was to transform Fourth Avenue from the open trench for steam trains that it was in 1903 to something grand.

* * *

PARK AVENUE—another example of nature being spotlighted by the great city; the city-teacher is clear about the significance and value of nature.

* * *

Wilgus, an engineer for the New York Central Railroad, and some other technicians who understood a thing or two about modernity and horniness, envisioned, committed to, then achieved the electrification of the trains. This event made the open trench obsolete. It was covered and new real estate was born.

Once Fourth Avenue had become a two-and-a-half-mile ramp, New York Central Railroad Company dressed things up with two parallel lines of fourteen- to sixteen-story apartment buildings. These original apartment buildings can be seen north of 57th Street. The street rapidly becomes one of the most expensive, most exclusive addresses on earth. These men were not only architects of material matter, they were also architects of perception.

New York Central originally owned Park Avenue because it

was the ramp leading to the new railroad terminal. One family owned New York Central Railroad at that time: the **Vanderbilts.** Hence, the Vanderbilts owned all of this. (**For more about the Vanderbilts, see "Wall Street: The Story of What Happened to Our Intimacy."**)

As we ascend Park Avenue, we are walking among the large, glass, commercial buildings that occupy the street today. Watch the traffic and the tumultuous feelings of significance/insignificance that infiltrate this reality. Notice the steel strips that cut across the street and sidewalk. Straddle these strips and wait for a truck or bus to drive over them. Feel the vibrations. This steel is part of this bridge!

Everything you see around you—the buildings, the dwellers of the buildings, all the dwellers' needs, all the mailmen, all the power lunches, even the taxicabs passing by and those who desperately try to flag one down—is occurring on a bridge, all of it, including ourselves, is vibrating all at once. Park Avenue is one vibration.

Vibration is a shared experience. It is a manifestation of interconnectedness. We are on earth to vibrate together. Every activity, no matter how diverse, contributes to the vibration of Park Avenue, contributes to the vibration of the Earth, contributes to the vibration of the universe.

If we were standing in a Midtown Manhattan that was a fully realized *home* and not an island of refugees, **all the people whom we have ever found boring will *suddenly be fascinating*.** Park Avenue would suddenly be a great stage for us to exist on eternally in that moment when forever loves of our lives decide to kiss us for the first time.

On the eastern side of **Park Avenue and 47th Street** there is a life-size statue of a man in a suit, flagging down a cab. He is so successfully naturalistic it takes some time to notice that he is art. A man flagging down a cab is art. My favorite sculptures are those that remind me that everything I do is art.

The name *Park Avenue* would make more sense if the park that originally lined the middle of the boulevard still existed. Fountain vistas and park benches surreptitiously placed to incite romances (and the end of romances) were once the centerpiece of this place.

Park Avenue is yet another example of Nature sneaking her way back onto the island, to make herself the center of attention disguised as an expensive celebration of botany. **(For more on Mother Nature understood as a cosmopolitan, refer to "Central Park: Mother Nature Is Cosmopolitan.")**

This whole dysfunction *that is currently* ***Park Avenue*** *is* ***a magic act*** *involving trees that disappear.* Therefore, we are strange trees.

Let's walk up a few blocks to **Park Avenue and 49th Street**. We see the **Waldorf-Astoria Hotel.**

This is the second version of the original Astor family hotel, which was located on 34th Street and Fifth Avenue, where the Empire State Building now stands. **(For more about this tale, see "A Tour of the Empire State Building Observation Deck Line.")**

Note the crack along the base of the Waldorf-Astoria Hotel, where the building meets the sidewalk. Directly across 49th Street, you'll notice a similiar crack between the **Intercontinental Hotel** and the sidewalk. They are shock absorbers designed to minimize the vibrations from the trains below. There are one hundred and sixty four railroad tracks beneath Park Avenue, on two levels.

A crack runs along the bottom of the Waldorf-Astoria Hotel;
it is a jigsaw piece fit into a
jigsaw puzzle.

In 1946, Grand Central Terminal and the tracks below Park Avenue became the busiest railroad terminal in the world. A train left one of Grand Central's platforms every thirty seconds, a powerful example of the enormous energy that emanated from this dreamscape called "America" as it rumbled toward superpower status.

When **Otto von Bismarck**, the great politician of the nineteenth century, was on his deathbed, he was asked to predict what the major geopolitical fact of the twentieth century would be. He answered, "North America speaks English." Grand Central Terminal is the exlamation point that follows his pronouncement.

And what was the twentieth century? *Isn't it really just a time right before a* larger version of **chocolate meets** a larger version of **peanut butter?** Is it, perhaps, the psychological proof we've needed to prove that Freud was a poet? Perhaps this century has been a minor disturbance in the force that is causing Obi Wan to barely twitch.

Let us take our visit to the interior of the Waldorf-Astoria. The front entrance has a pearly white sensation, a "what a brave new world, with such characters in it" kind of feeling.

Up the red stairs, we walk into a permanent morning. The mosaic on the floor is the portrayal of a random, rural scene. It is daylight forever. We may or may not be in Germany. All the objects here are permanently laminated with a thick coat of German baroque expressionism.

As you move toward the elevators, morning becomes afternoon. **The afternoon will always look the same here.** There are shops and a bar, pictures on the wall. Now it is evening.

The restaurant is permanent night descending on permanent day. **Peacock Alley** got its name from the famous alleyway that used to connect the original Astor mansions on 34th Street and Fifth Avenue. Peacock Alley was a place to be seen in a stylish age. This is where F. Scott Fitzgerald first learned how to articulate mistrust. (**For more about this, see "A Tour of the Empire State Building Observation Deck Line."**)

I stood in this room recently with an astrophysicist named **Mark Vagans**. We began our tour of each other when he announced, **"I'm a scientist who specializes in the END OF THE UNIVERSE."**

He stood in this room and explained to me that **neutrinos** are the stardust of heavenly bodies falling through the universe, and they are more numerous than anything else in the universe—even McDonald's. Vagans is experimentation: the attempt to weigh a neutrino. He wants to know if weight is a sensation the neutrinos feel.

Vagan's words soared through the Waldorf lobby. Neutrinos were flying through our bodies at the speed of light. "If neutrinos have weight," he said, "we're living in a universe that recycles itself, but if neutrinos are weightless the universe is *limitless*."

"I'm rooting for the limitlessness," I replied.

I assure you, the word limitlessness is not just an assortment of well-meaning syllables; it is a declaration of ***WAR against all BOUNDARIES.***

Exit the Waldorf-Astoria Hotel back onto the **Park Avenue** side, and walk across **49th Street.**

On the right, in the distance, on **53rd Street and Park Avenue,** you'll see the **Seagram Building.** It is the black, monolithic building on the east side of the street. Designed by **Mies van der Rohe and Philip Johnson**, the Seagram Building looks like many other buildings in Midtown Manhattan today, but it was the first of its kind.

Through trial and error, Manhattanites came to understand

how to zone tall buildings so that sunlight could shine onto their streets. There are streets in Lower Manhattan that, as part of that process, will never see sunlight again.

The **zoning law of 1916** insisted that the taller the building, the farther back it must be set (to create space between itself and the sidewalk). This is why so many buildings in Midtown Manhattan look like giant wedding cakes or Sumerian ziggurats. The buildings have to push themselves backward and inward as they rise. The result: a vast array of terraces, loggias, and other indentations.

The Seagram Building is one of the originalities created by the 1916 legislation. Mies van der Rohe pulled the entire building away from the sidewalk and shot it straight up into the sky, a single stream of materials that open a space on the ground for a sidewalk-expanding plaza and the possibility for sunlight to kiss the asphalt jungle.

Roll farther west along 49th Street. Cross Park Avenue to the beyond-chic zone. We are cruising toward **Madison Avenue.** Soon we will be confronted by the store started by **Bernard Saks** in 1933, on West 34th Street. Today it is known as **Saks Fifth Avenue.** Peer into the infamous Saks Fifth Avenue windows and OBSERVE THE MANNEQUINS POSING. Which part of you identifies with them? **(For more about shopping and fashion, see "A Tour of Bloomingdales: Suffering Is an Addiction to Self-Doubt . . . Maybe.")**

On the next corner, across the street from Saks Fifth Avenue, is **St. Patrick's Cathedral.**

Visiting St. Patrick's Cathedral is an especially transcendent experience when one recognizes that our visit adds to the cathedral's feeling of being an important landmark. Look up at the terrific spires shooting over a hundred feet into the sky, and feel the arch of your back echoing the shape of the building. *We look good, and our breathing and our style are major contributions to this scene.*

Before we even enter the cathedral doors, we have a transcendent experience waiting for us on the stairs that lead to the entrance. They are literally "uplifting." As pedestrians we spend so much time on the sidewalk that it is a rare and fascinating opportunity to stand at the top of this staircase. This city becomes a giant novel and suddenly we are omniscient narrators. Standing at this height, it is easy to see the unconscious poetic collaboration between people.

Watch how the guy unloading a truck full of eggs is carrying a tray of them into a store where a pregnant woman is working behind the counter. Note how people walking fast *need* the people who walk slow in order to feel fast. Experience fully the spotlight that the man directing traffic must feel and *feel entirely the* ***salaciousness*** *shared between a* ***hot-dog vendor*** *and the* ***hunger of passersby.***

Compare the enormous towers of **Rockefeller Center**, across the street, to the cathedral's spires. As grandiose and beautiful as St. Patrick's is, or any of the other places of worship along these streets, notice how they are dwarfed by buildings where business is done. Inside St. Patrick's Cathedral, God and transcendence are being openly prayed to and felt, yet walking back outside the cathedral is to feel the reduction of its significance on this boulevard.

Joseph Campbell, an anthropological cruiser, observed that the priorties of a place and its people can be easily discerned by their tallest buildings. In the Middle Ages, the church was the tallest structure. In the Renaissance, the palace and other residences of note became the tallest. In modern cities, office buildings win hands down.

New York City is European history *on cocaine.* The Middle Ages took place over a weekend, the Renaissance was a holiday, and the **Industrial Revolution** happened one day when **Rockefeller sneezed.** Trinity Church was the tallest structure in the city only a hundred and twenty years ago. In the 1880s, it was the Brooklyn Bridge. The World Trade Towers, while they stood, were the ultimate symbol of New York's priorities. They were buildings that represented altitude for altitude's sake. "Growth for the sake of growth," Edward Abbey once said, "is the ideology of a cancer cell." Now that they are gone, one wonders what the next architectural articulation of ourselves and our culture might look like. We've been thrust back in time—our totem, the Empire State Building—living the articulation of time long ago. *To see what goes up next in that SIXTEEN-ACRE HAUNTED ZONE will tell you everything you need to know about our COLLECTIVE FUTURE.*

Standing in the middle of Fifth Avenue is modern man's Roman Forum fantasy, Rockefeller Center.

As an adolescent, having spent eighteen years dwelling awkwardly among people who were trying to convince me that I was insane, Rockefeller Center seemed Grecian to me. Its dedication to symmetry, to balance, is noticeable. It seemed to me a "middle way." The entire esplanade created by the buildings of Rockefeller Center sanctified pleasantness, a **homeostasis** sitting pretty in the middle of great *tumultuousness.* From the point of view of me and my disarray, Rockefeller Center was the epitome of centeredness.

I landed an internship at a production office in one of the Rockefeller Center buildings when I was twenty-one. A student studying playwriting in a culture that had decreed theater obsolete, I was told by someone that I had to find a niche in society. It was confusing. I would walk off the subway into the infinite subterranean corridor below Rockefeller Center that stretches between Fifth Avenue and Sixth Avenue, and claims to be the personification of empire. The twisting and turning hallways all lead to the colosseum floor. Eventually, I went insane in that Roman travesty and decided that being a playwright in modern America was going to be my niche in society. I was thus a "lost soul."

When Midtown Manhattan becomes a *home* and not a macabre orgy of unconscious scavengers the word *normal* will become obsolete.

Rockefeller Center's enormous terraces are designed to be gardens, some of them sitting fifty floors above the sidewalk. These are ***the hanging gardens of Babylon reborn.*** Note the twin ziggurats greeting you at the main entrance. A pseudo-Mycenaean lion's gate on the north wall of the esplanade and the pseudo-Zeus peering down on us, complete with lightning bolts, from **30 Rockefeller Center's** entranceway are other examples of the ancient allusions to be found here. This is the restoration of Nebuchadrezzar's dynasty; he mops the floors after everyone has gone home. Hammurabi is a conductor on the subway down below. ***"An eye for an eye, a tooth for a tooth" is still the essential law of this land.***

Note, too, the large golden statue of **Prometheus** lounging over Rockefeller Center's famous sunken plaza that becomes an ice-skating rink in the winter. As a punishment for bringing fire to mankind, Prometheus was chained to a rock so his liver could be eaten by crows. His liver would grow back, and the crows would return to eat it again. All he wanted was for us to take responsibility for our fire.

The gold Prometheus hovering above the Rockefeller Center ice-skating rink is one of the major icons of twentieth-century America. What is this thing we call the twentieth century? I am standing here at the bitter, nonchalant end of a bedlam, a carnage, and what has certainly been a giant self-reflection.

Self-reflection is the electrical current surging between us and our interconnection to every living thing. **Confusion** is the state of being electrified by this electrical current.

PROMETHEUS—*TORTURED*
because he wanted us to take responsibility for our own fire . . .

We are involved with an incomprehensible process that, however messy, is nonetheless a process. The reason I am so sure of this: I wake up and find the world still here every afternoon. When I consider the amount of turmoil and murder brimming and brewing within the average person, it seems to me a miracle that the world has not been blown up. Perhaps it will happen. But for the time being, it has not, and this is all the proof I need to believe in us.

Can you hear the full-throttled cacophony of this tempestuous yet somehow average moment in Midtown Manhattan? All the noise listened to at once produces the same sound of unity and wholeness that Siddhartha heard when he listened to the Ganges River in its entirety. This great teacher that is the city is crying out to you right now. It is crying out, **"Om."**

The city resonates with the same universal sound that the Ganges rings with because there is no difference between the city and the universe except that the city is where we dwell in the universe.

In America, they say there is ***a murder every twelve seconds,*** **a dishwasher finishing its cycle every ten seconds,** ***a broken nail every half nanosecond,*** but they never seem to get around to mentioning that *enlightenment happens on a continuum basis.*

Enlightenment happens every time your friend feels depressed and you become depressed to keep him or her company. (**For more about depression, see "A Tour of Washington Square Park and My Heart: Fear Is Joy Paralyzed."**)

Enlightenment happens whenever one swan is hungry but notices another swan is ill and so does not eat all the food but rather aids his or her sick swan friend.

It happens whenever a Yankee hits a home run in the Bronx.

It happens whenever a roller-blader stumbles and falls and another roller-blader rolls up to help him.

In Midtown Manhattan enlightenment moves faster than a rigged taxi meter.

And so my question is this: If the interconnectedness of all life on earth is a given, and loneliness *really is a delusion*, how come I miss Natasha-at-Times-Simone so much?

A conundrum.

If Gaea were in full fruition right now, you would be able to fall deeply in love with everyone you meet in the new Disney store on 42nd Street and everyone would fall in love with you.

Close your eyes and listen to Times Square swarming around you. Sense and allow your sensitivity to grow, in this moment. **Try to hear all the sounds of Times Square at once. You will start to hear the universe's way of life: OM.**

A Tour of the Lower East Side: You Are a Better Party than Any Party Ever

Depression is the surest way to evil.
—Rabbi Nachman

I came in here for a special offer—guaranteed personality.
—The Clash

The dream is to be loved for who we really are. A **label** happens whenever laziness and language hang out and have a beer. Let's go back to a time before we had labels, laziness, or language. On this tour, we visit an imaginary neighborhood that was all too real a hundred years ago, we visit with our ancestors and we can hear our great-great-grandmothers demanding from beyond the grave that we shave!

Gravity is all over my ass. It's all over yours, too. When sensitive astronauts orbit the planet and view our big blue ball with their own two eyes, they re-enter the atmosphere laughing at the notion of nations and cultures. They no longer feel Cuban or American or Russian; they are universal.

Let's you and me float together for a while without any labels.

THE LOWER EAST SIDE: an opportunity to float together without names.

Our differences will become beauty instead of war as long as we are united by the common shared thrill of being alive.

If the whole world would behave like the **Lower East Side**, the whole world would become Beauty-Never-War.

Sensitive astronauts come CRASHING back into the atmosphere *laughing* at the notion of nations.

At the turn of the nineteenth century, the Lower East Side was no longer a neighborhood. It became a reservoir for humanity. Tribes and ethnicities and nationalities that have been at war for the last two thousand years are suddenly on the B train together and living down the hallway from each other.

This event called "New York City" is actually the jangling of many ancient torments and agonies healing together. **When one considers how many "enemies" are cohabitating here, one soon realizes that *New York City is a place of great harmony.***

There is alienation in New York City. Yet it is a shared alienation. **(For more about shared alienation, refer to "The Midtown Rush Hour Tour").**

There is an average of twelve families living per tenement floor. There are three bathtubs for every thirteen hundred families. This challenge to hygiene leads to the erection of public bathhouses. Immigrants were slotted for weekly baths and given free bars of soap by the newly invented Public Health Department.

The Lower East Side is, relatively speaking, a ghost town these days. It is still feeling sore after the exercise of an exuberant migration. Today we will have to reinvent a massive neighborhood in our minds and then walk the streets. ***A tour of the Lower East Side today is as much a tour of the imagination as it is of any actual place.***

Therefore, I have designed a psychedelic trip for you to trip into so we can be the beings we were before our parents named us while visiting with our ancestors.

Imagine imaginary tabs of acid and take the imaginary tabs of sacred medicine that your imagination has imaginatively imagined for you and place the imaginary tabs in the center of your palm between the love and intelligence lines. May these imaginary tabs melt all the masks you have worn in this life thus far lived, and dwarf all the labels the world outside of yourself has placed on you, and may they bring you back to the original "Good night! Good night! Parting is such sweet sorrow, that I shall say good night till it be morrow."

On the topic of genealogy, remember this: **YOU ARE THE CURRENT, WALKING CLIMAX OF YOUR ENTIRE FAMILY TREE.**

Welcome to the Lower East Side!

WE BEGIN AT RUTGERS STREET AND EAST BROADWAY: THE CORNER OF THE F-TRAIN STOP:

Let's start with the living before dealing with the ghosts and head into Chinatown by going east along East Broadway. This is the semi-vast byway running rampant with transactions of every stripe and adventures in gregariousness that finds its origin below the blue Manhattan Bridge (completed in 1907).

Commingle and share some present tense with eel-filled tanks and the countless suffocating crabs stuffed in brown paper bags, and groove with the elderly Chinese women playing checkers in a star. These are the people of **Canton**, which was absorbed by China during the Tung Dynasty of 619 A.D.

According to the census, there were 150 Chinese people here in 1859. By 1890, there were 110,000 and 3.5 percent were women. The American government, in a dramatic gesture of anti-Cruise, would not allow Chinese women into the country, and so **the CHINESE MEN of this city endured one of the l o n g e s t d r y s p e l l s of all time.** The American policy was focused on disallowing the Chinese the possibility of procreating on this continent.

After walking in and out of some stores and moving up and down a few sidewalks, return to **East Broadway and Rutgers** and look westward. Unlike the immigrants of these streets one hundred years ago, the Chinese are not interested in becoming Americanized, and so looking eastward from this intersection is a true look to the east. Looking westward is truly a return to Western civilization.

The almost-square we stand on is named after **Nathan Straus**, a Jewish philanthropist who brought free sterilized-milk stations to the children of America. The ingestion of another animal's milk has now relieved mothers of the responsibility of breast-feeding and the latter-day creation of formula with all its attendant propaganda-cum-advertising has succeeded in introducing artificial substances to human existence from day one. I, myself, Timothy "Speed" Levitch, am a victim of this corporate conspiracy. Thanks Mr. Straus!

I spend most of my money on LAP DANCES because I was NOT BREAST-FED.

Nathan Straus, partner to R. H. Macy, was a philanthropist whose philanthropy tore us from the warmth of our mother's breasts. (**See also "A Tour of Ladies Mile: Women Are Life."**) Straus, along with poverty and disease, are forces that helped invent the special brand of immigrant-neurotic whose supra-paranoid view of the world would flood their children's generation and eventually reach its apogee in the creation of **Woody Allen**.

St. Theresa's Church, a triangular church sitting on the southeast corner of **East Broadway and Rutgers**, is a place where you can still hear the prayers of survivors of the Irish potato famine. This is a Gothic revival from the 1840s, whose corporal stone and altar was converted to Catholicism in the 1860s when the Irish flood became irresistible. Today, St. Theresa's is an architectural editorial on the topic of transition. The services in this church are conducted in Spanish, English, and Chinese. Three different languages that landed here from three different directions, three different tribes praying to three different Gods, and yet all coming here for the same reason—to satisfy hunger.

The **parking lot** next to St. Theresa's Church has a new condo on it called "149 Crossroads." It is thus a representative of the area's gentrification. The landed gentry, the young newly upwardly wealthy, are arriving in the old Lower East Side to claim it as a new, hip location for residing and investing well. ***The turmoil of the recent past is suddenly a good investment. These are the complicated jokes the great comedian, New York City, loves to tell.*** (**See also, "We Do Not Fear Death As Much As We Fear Immortality: Madison Square Park."**)

Across the street from St. Theresa's, on the northeast corner of Rutgers and East Broadway, is the Wing Shun Chinese restaurant, once the **Garden Cafeteria**. For decades, the Garden

Cafeteria was a vortex for Jewish intellectuals, thespians, and other constitutional outsiders.

You can hear the echo of their various inspirations reverberate to this day in the same way you can still hear the transcendentalists of the early nineteenth century just above the noise of America's factories.

Half a block up East Broadway is the **Jewish Forward Building.** It is the tall, white façade facing East Broadway. At the peak of the Jewish occupation of the Lower East Side there were over two hundred Yiddish publications churned out here. The *Forward* had the largest circulation.

Watch carefully the frieze portraits of Lenin, Trotsky, and Marx that line the opening cornice above the front entrance. You are standing at the portal where hardcore socialism reentered mainstream American culture for the first time since the **Homestead Act of 1840.**

On dark, lonely nights, the frieze of TROTSKY reminisces about the day he was ASSASSINATED in Mexico. He was stabbed with an ice pick but it did not kill him immediately. In fact, he had a few hours to get cozy with death. He was taken to his wife. They made love until the end. Trotsky was the embodiment of revolutionary fervor to the orgasmic end.

The *Forward*'s most famous shtick was a column called **Bintel Briefs**, which means "a bundle of letters." The *Forward*'s head-editor, **Abraham Cahan**, would take on rabbinical tones as he answered questions and tried to heal the grievances mailed in by his loyal, downtrodden immigrant readers. Questions like ***"My boss is a capitalist and I'm a communist, but I think he's a great guy. What should I do?"*** and "We live on the streets right now. I just had my fifth child. This wonderful couple has offered us a room in their apartment to live in, but the lady wants my fifth child. Is this what Americans mean by the term *barter*?" and "Why are all the agnostics I know frigid?"

Seward Park on the other side of the almost-square was **a desperate attempt to bring botany and ventilation to an area where stagnant air was omniscient and lethal.**

This park is an example of New York City's inventiveness as it attempted to find ways to make these streets a livable neighborhood. New York City was the first American city to be overwhelmed by homelessness, incompetency, crime, corruption, disease, insanity and potholes. This enormous trial-and-error process was the city's rite of passage that resulted in it becoming the first modern American city. **Bellevue Medical Center**, the first public hospital of the United States, invented the emergency room and the ambulance as the population around it invented new kinds of emergencies.

The **Educational Alliance**, which sits another block to the north at the corner of **East Broadway and Jefferson Street**, invented the first summer camp when it was faced with long summers filled with mass urban hysteria and unsupervised children.

However, the true goal of the Educational Alliance was **assimilation.**

What is my name? Whatever it is, it is an example of something that may or may not have anything to do with me. **ON MY BEST DAYS, I HAVE BEEN** NAMELESS. I've never been too close with the man I am supposed to be because I've never been able to just hang with that guy. My identity is the most draining and demanding caretaker relationship in my life.

Assimilation, a special flavor of agony, is the action of walking out on our own party in order to get invited to trendier parties. It is taking a step away from our true selves in order to become conformists—those who forget who they are in order to get invited to the right parties.

CONFORMITY IS FLUFFING UP PILLOWS FOR YOUR FEARS, MAKING THEM FEEL COMFORTABLE AND AT HOME IN THE LIVING ROOM OF YOUR LIFE.

The Education Alliance was one of several cultural and educational landmarks created by German Jews who had arrived fifty years before their ragged, embarrassing Eastern European cousins washed up on the shoreline. The scholarship practiced here was Americanism. There were classes teaching the young immigrant how to dress like an American, cook like an American, and speak proper American English.

Who are we? Any dogmatic answer is highly suspicious. My answer, merely a tour guide's tactic to ignite the inner stirring, emanates from my attempts to bravely tour and microscopically appreciate this **ongoing wow** that we call, for the sake of convenience, *reality.* When I am cruising it is obvious to me that our true selves are the greatest parties ever thrown.

How is your trip going so far? Are the imaginary tabs of boundary-dissolving psychotropics kicking in yet? Are you noticing that ***reality*** as a term possesses **no more validity than *Jordache*** or ***Baskin-Robbins?*** These labels are mouth noises emanating from a quiver in our esophaguses that we equate with the by-product process, which is our true pursuit of self and meaning. These labels exist to help move the afternoon along and to abridge our thinking and our feelings about what is really going on.

As we stroll past the Educational Alliance, notice that only by allowing our fear of other people's opinions about us to take over our lives can we be reduced to such diluted simulations of ourselves. The invisible language of status can only be spoken through other people's mouths. (**See Madison Avenue advertisement firms.**)

The local branch of the New York Public Library, which faces the Educational Alliance on the other side of East Broadway, opened in 1910. This library was a major destination for the Jewish immigrants of the Lower East Side. There are photographs of enormous lines that would form at the front entrance. Hundreds would wait to enter just like the ancient Jewish population of Alexandria, Egypt, with its world-famous library standing as though it were so many signposts for the Diaspora community. **THE DAY THE FAMOUS LIBRARY OF ALEXANDRIA BURNED DOWN** IS AN INTERNATIONAL HOLIDAY FOR ALL THOSE WHO **SUFFER FOR KNOWLEDGE.**

As we move farther up East Broadway, note the synagogues planted in the basements and first floors of the apartment buildings. The **Young Israel Synagogue** is one of the more prominent ones to be seen along the sidewalk, a young orthodox Jewish congregation founded in 1913 to combat the growth of *Reform Judaism.*

Reform Judaism was a new practice of Judaism invented in the **Enlightenment** that found its first full existence among the German Jews who landed here after the revolution of 1848. The first reform Jewish temples grew up on these streets along with the newest kind of Jews living entirely innovative lives, at least when you compare them to their immediate ancestors.

The traditional Jewish communities who entirely adhere to the ways of the ancestors also pray here. In many chabbads around this neighborhood, Lubavitcher Jews celebrate the Messiah's recent return in the body of a man named Schneerson. In these nearby corridors, the Jewish exile is kaput, the promise delivered to Abraham and his descendants unveiled.

At East Broadway and Montgomery Streets, turn right onto

Henry Street. To your left, across the street, you will find the Henry Street Settlement. The settlement is housed in a trio of Federal-style row houses whose upkeep is almost ostentatious compared to most buildings in the area. Essentially a delivery service of nurses, the Henry Street Settlement was invented by Lillian Wald—a nurse appalled by the dearth of medical aid in the Lower East Side of 1893.

NEW YORK CITY SPEAKS THE LANGUAGE OF DELIVERY. Every time a pizza or a plate of Chinese broccoli is delivered to an apartment the city is actually happening as the interconnectedness of the human race is being directly experienced. The Henry Street Settlement did not deliver beer or videos to the tenements of the Lower East Side; they delivered healing.

The Henry Street Settlement:
NYC's first delivery service–
delivering nurses and intimate health care
and blazing forth the path for many
future deliveries of **pizza**
and **Chinese food.**

The next door neighbor of this philanthropic landmark is a fire house. In 1854, it was a volunteer fire department known as *Americus 6*. Can you feel the energy of the landmark fire station that was the launching pad for the career of the greatest and most corrupt politician of New York's municipal history, **William Marcy "Boss" Tweed?**

The original fire departments of the city formed the original caucuses of the democratic process in New York. They were gangs with fire hoses. There are famous anecdotes of two rival fire departments showing up at the same fire and engaging in fistfights to decide who would put out the fire, while the building burns in the background. Visualize this scene and you are viewing *democracy in its purest form—a fistfight over a fire.*

Most major Irish politicians of the nineteenth century in New York City—and these were some of the most powerful politicians in the history of the city—began their political careers as volunteer firemen.

Boss Tweed was one of these pure emanations, a collection of extreme events and living conditions, which created a versatile politician who turned the city into a dictatorship and transformed all city planning into self-expression. **IT IS ESTIMATED THAT BY THE TIME OF HIS ARREST, TWEED HAD STOLEN FORTY-FIVE MILLION DOLLARS, IN 1870S MONEY, FROM NEW YORK CITY.**

Poetically, the only landmark to survive with Tweed's name on it is a courthouse, a classical structure sitting behind City Hall. Constructed in 1872, it was originally supposed to cost New York City six hundred thousand dollars to construct. It ended up costing twelve million dollars.

If the anti-Cruise doesn't stop you at the portal, note the painting of a tiger on the side wall of the fire station. **Thomas Nast**, the cartoonist who invented today's image of **Santa Claus**, created this tiger to describe the attitude and tempo of **Tammany Hall**, the Irish political headquarters.

The tiger is still growling, tribalism—the only true religion of all people—can still be felt on these streets. Any fair election today is a slap in the face of the past because the nod and wink of yore has gone backstage. This is why **MOST IMMIGRANT GROUPS EVENTUALLY EQUATE THE AMERICAN DREAM WITH ORGANIZED CRIME.** The important things never change.

Five Points, one of the initial New York Irish neighborhoods, just north of City Hall, was an overpopulated marshland that bred malaria, proffered frozen deaths in the winter, and sired great municipal politicians.

The Italians that were coming over in greater numbers later in the century arrived to find that the Irish had already seized the bureaucracy of Catholicism. The two ethnicities had different visions of Catholicism, and the Irish were in charge of the whole enchilada. **St. Ann's Church** at **70 Mott Street** was a famous Catholic church of that time. It made room for the Italians on Sunday mornings by cleaning out the basements. That their belief in God did not find comfortable quarters in the New World mirrors the treacherous journey that faced all Italian immigrants. The most hyperbolic attempts these immigrants made to muscle their way into the inner circles of American power have produced many Hollywood movie classics.

Today, what is called **Little Italy** is actually just **Mulberry Street** and the side streets that branch off of Mulberry. This sanitized area tells the Hallmark-card version of the Italian story.

We are getting more lost—the trip is kicking in. There is an alleyway behind the children's fenced-in playground. Turn right. Suddenly, you are on **Grand Street**, farther west it becomes a delicate and stylish street of SoHo, but at this longitude it is a magical passageway. When we return to East Broadway, we will find an ornate classical building looking awkwardly upon this intersection of unornamented buildings. This was originally the **Young Christian Brotherhood**. Today it is a mikvah—an ancient bathhouse filled with sacred rituals for the cleansing of Jewish men and women.

Can you *imagine* this building's *confusion?* Can you imagine the different spectrums of humanity this building has associated with? It was built to house young men and their aspiration to be good Christians. It was sold into the hands of Jews and now houses an ancient ritual bent on the dubious aspiration to be clean.

This building, more than any of us, is a true New Yorker.

Across East Broadway, the **Bialystoker Synagogue** at **7 Willet Street** is a good example of an 1820s Methodist church that converted to Judaism (in 1905). By the mid-1890s, there were over five hundred synagogues in the Lower East Side of Manhattan. This is one of the few active ones remaining. People think that people are the only ones who convert religions, but in the Lower East Side the buildings do it all the time.

The synagogue faces west because it was originally a church and at that time had no interest in facing east. Synagogues traditionally face east, toward Jerusalem. When this Methodist-church-turned-Bialystoker-Synagogue someday becomes a Chinese Buddhist temple or a Haitian seminary for Catholic priests, it will still be facing the wrong direction.

How is your trip going? Are the imaginary tabs of imagination encroaching upon the autonomous part of your mind? **Take a moment of significance as the mind oil kisses** insignificance. **Stand and** witness yourselflost and anonymous.

Walk down to **Pitt Street** and take a right. On your left is the **local police precinct**, but it doesn't matter. In our current consciousness, these are merely human beings in carefully designed costumes caught up in an enormous improvisation. **These are God's puppets forgetting their puppeteer, masters with masks so adept with masks that they have forgotten they are wearing masks.** It was only recently in New York City history that the police department started advertising itself as anything other than the mayor's private army.

The New York Police Department continues to wrestle with knowing who it really is just as we all do. Our **identity** is the major caretaker relationship of our lives. Of all our relationships, it is by far the most enervating. I have fallen off cliff sides with weepy, needy women, but none of them were as impossible to satisfy and in as constant need of my unswerving attention as my identity.

If we follow Pitt Street to the end, we will eventually be standing underneath the **Williamsburg Bridge**. One of the three major bridges along with the Brooklyn and Manhattan, that would help millions of immigrants escape the overcrowded Lower East Side into Brooklyn and Queens. Note the enormous ramp leading to the bridge, above us and moving a mile inland from here. Imagine how many **tenements** were destroyed to make way for this land bridge. ***Imagine all the families that spilled out onto the street, desperate.***

There had been virtually no attempts to regulate the tenements before 1879.

The law passed in 1879 required that an air shaft be built between consecutive tenements. The law required that staircases be wider and constructed of fireproof materials, and that there be **A TOILET FOR EVERY TWO APARTMENTS.** For the first time, water was piped into each room. The law of 1879 altered the basic shape of the basic Lower East Side tenement; no longer simple rectangles, they became shaped like enormous exercise *dumbbells.* These tenements are commonly referred to as *dumbbell tenements.* **(For more about tenements and their story, go to the Tenement Museum at 97 Orchard Street.)**

On **Delancey Street**, turn left. On the corner is a storefront window of caged chickens awaiting slaughter. This land was Delancey's farm in the late eighteenth century. **Division Street**, a diagonal street running through the Lower East Side, was the original fence dividing Delancey's farm from **Rutger's farm.** Delancey was exiled from the United States at the end of the American Revolutionary War because he was a royalist who had housed British soldiers during their conquest of the city.

(For more about the Revolutionary War, see "Central Park: Mother Nature Is Cosmopolitan.")

At **Delancey and Attorney Streets**, we take a right up Attorney and halfway down the block find an empty parking lot with part of a brick wall, the western wall, still standing. This place, the **Congregation of the Shield of Abraham**, was destroyed by fire. The western wall is the only thing left. The Jews here fled. They were not running from conquering Romans this time; they were running toward more valuable real estate uptown.

Standing in front of the rubble that was once the Congregation of the Shield of Abraham, we are standing with the rubble of all of our attempts to be the person others say we should be. **The true underlying mantra chanted all day by a good citizen is, "EVERYONE ELSE KNOWS WHO I AM SUPPOSED TO BE MORE THAN I DO."**

Take a moment here to admit that you know the roles you play better than you know yourself.

To become a *policeman* or a *French maid* is merely to become a theatrical role; being ourselves is *bliss.* Our exuberance is an even more mythological figure than the immigrants who first crossed this bridge, because it comes from a place much farther away than Europe. Yet the immigrant entering the Lower East Side of Manhattan traveled the same arc as their exuberances did in this world. They enter these streets thrilled to be here and then, instantly, face desecrations of spirit such as sixteen-hour days for ten cents a day in sweatshops, or being shot down on an abandoned dockside in a gangster-style assassination. **(For more on the murder of our exuberance, see the society we live in.)**

The immigrant is an adult who has been given a renewed hope for joy in mid-adulthood. **Immigration** is the understanding that **adulthood is an opportunity to do childhood one better.**

At the next corner, **Attorney Street** intersects with **Rivington Street.** This street is named after one of the patron saints of the Lower East Side who was sanctified because of his lack of identifiability. This man, supposedly named Rivington, was a spy during the American Revolutionary War, and for the last two hundred years was considered a traitor. Due to a recent discovery of certain documents, historians have now concluded that Rivington was, in fact, a double agent. He is now considered a hero.

On Rivington, just west of **Norfolk Street**, is **Streit's Matzoh Factory**, which bakes its goods in an active Dominican and Puerto Rican community. This is a rustic operation producing ancient matter, co-existing with vivacious Latins. As we stand among these shelves of unleavened bread for sale, I would like to dedicate this moment of the tour to **Moses**—the tour guide who overcame self-doubt and a less than accommodating tour route. **Matzoh was invented by slaves racing toward freedom.** It will taste righteous to those of us attempting to escape into our true selves.

How is your trip going? If you are still able to muster an interest in destinations and the concept of having destinations, then please turn right at Norfolk Street. On the way to the first Reform Jewish temple in American history, become someone else and then become that someone else's lover. ***Notice how much easier it is to view everything around you as new and as an ongoing astonishment, because you are new and an ongoing astonishment.*** Perhaps the only reason to be interested in lineage is to liberate ourselves from its self-propelled illusions.

Anche Chesed is the dark-red stucco façade we pass while **walking north on Norfolk Street, right before we reach Houston Street.** Anshe Chesed is the first Reform Jewish temple in American history. The building appears, in places, to be crumbling under the sheer weight of this.

A building cannot be the first Reform Jewish temple in American if it does not know the sensation of crumbling.

In the façade of the Anche Chesed Temple, Jews have reproduced the façade of the Cologne Cathedral then miniaturized it and painted it red; some façades are also allegories.

Inside Anche Chesed, the main sanctuary looks like it has just been promoted to the rank of archaeological find. Composed of wood and mildew, the central ark could also be the central ark of a synagogue aboard a sunken ocean liner. The balcony that rings the second floor, originally reserved for the women of the congregation, now turns the whole room into a scene from some invention by Edgar Allen Poe.

As we stand in this place of worship let us compute the infinitesimal odds, the wandering coincidences, and the earnest drunken accidents that brought the Jews in such numbers to these streets. *If human history is a collection of pornographic moments, the Jewish Diaspora is an early centerfold*. For a thousand years the Jews of central Europe and Russia had existed in an enforced boundary called the Pale of Settlement which was a stretch of impoverished towns, called shtetls, where the Jews lived out tortured lives, generation after generation.

Among the bloodshed, Russian rabbis asked their congregations to remain in Russia and warned against going to America. In America, it was argued, the Jews would lose their souls.

Jews have been dispersed throughout the world. God wants them to feel at home everywhere. Also, God wants all the other tribes of the world to feel at home with them. The Diaspora is an ongoing possibility for the Jews to notice that they can see God from anywhere they stand.

The melted Pale of Settlement rebuilt itself along these streets of New York's Lower East Side, and it is certainly a cosmic occasion that the czar of Russia pronounced open hunting season on the Jews just as America's doors were being opened to the persecuted masses of the world. America's doors would not stay open for long.

Two and a half million European Jews landed in the Lower East Side of New York at the turn of the century. To find another population of that size in the history of the Jews, one must trace backward in time to Alexandria, Egypt, under the rule of Ptolemy soon after the rise and fall of Alexander the Great. (**For more on Alexander the Great, see "A Tour of the Empire State Building Observation Deck Line."**)

This is not some historically accurate fact unearthed to grace the pages of a textbook. The city is a mythological event. We call this event happening around us New York City, but that is a label and an example of language being used to enable vagueness. *Zeus refers to this place as "a direct hit!"* Truthfully, I do not know what to call it, but I'm glad to be part of it.

Move north to **Houston and Norfolk.** Across the street there is a condominium called *Red Square.* A real Moscow statue of Comrade Lenin is saluting you from the roof. The statue is backlit at night. **REAL ESTATE SPECULATION CAN THUS BE FOUND USING THE RADICAL'S CRY TO ERASE ALL NOTIONS OF PROPERTY TO SELL PROPERTY.**

Two blocks directly west, on the corner of **Houston and Ludlow Streets,** is **Katz's Delicatessen.** Head toward Katz's and as you walk along Houston Street, note the lack of building façades here. This is one of several streets in New York City that was widened. These buildings have all had their façades blown off to make way for the twentieth century in general. The Lower East Side is the city's melodrama meant to explode façades.

Inside Katz's Deli is the food of a certain ethnic story narrating itself through flavor. It is a place that has been entirely *eaten in.* The butchers behind the counter are celebrities here. Katz's is famous for its egg creams, its aura, and its hot dogs.

The hot dog, invented in Coney Island in 1884, is the world's first true postmodern expression. It is a sample of many ingredients brought together to invent a new taste.

If you travel three more blocks eastward along Houston Street, you come to **Orchard Street.** This street is famous for its **bargains.** A bargain is the interruption of expectation. There is a whole plantation of these interruptions of expectation waiting for us on Orchard Street.

How is your trip going? Are the imaginative tabs you took sending you ballistically into adventures that lead back to yourself? Can you feel yourself being sighted as an unidentified flying object in some far-off, far more advanced galaxy? Does the question asked at all lame parties, ***"What do you do?"***, seem unanswerable for all time?

Are you standing on **Orchard Street**, becoming your own cocktail party, *in* with the *in crowd,* just by standing still?

A Tour of the Cathedral of St. John the Divine: Cathedral Party

Don't forget to laugh at the world.
—Parmahansa Yogananda

Why do I only feel Christian indoors?
—Alan Watts

The **Cathedral of St. John the Divine,** on most days, is a ***giant art installation*** unaware of itself because it still thinks that it's a **contruction site.** It is quite incredible to walk down the colossal colonnade of this godly place surrounded by dull, nonsmiling people who are, right before your eyes, living out the act of totally losing sight of the miracle of being alive. Then to turn a corner and be met by a person in deep contemplation and prayer, kneeling before an ancient artifact while convening with the infinite, and all of this happening on 110th Street and Amsterdam Avenue. (**For more on prayer for the human race's**

future, refer to "A Tour of Bloomingdale's: Suffering Is an Addiction to Self-Doubt . . . Maybe.")

Any argument is a conversation about vitality and the **Cruise** is the ongoing attempt to constantly appreciate God's sense of humor. My faith in God, which came after discovering new esoteric sex positions, and after I noticed that all my suffering was making me sexier and funnier, greatly improved my tour of the Cathedral of St. John the Divine.

Fun is a form of **faith; faith** is active **fun**. Fun is the act of coitus lifted into the air of the universe in the guise of quotidian ecstasy, and ***we can have fun WITHOUT LIFTING A FINGER due to this magical power called faith.***

Welcome to the Cathedral of St. John the Divine!

In the garden to the south of the **Cathedral of St. John the Divine** there is a fountain that appears to have lost its mind. It is shaped like a monstronsity and the statuary is actually a pile of crazed beings intertwined and on top of each other. The piece is entitled "**Peace Fountain.**" It was sculpted by **Greg Wyatt** and it is dedicated to the children of the world. The plaque reads, "Peace Fountain celebrates the triumph of good or evil . . . when the fountain operates, four courses of water cascade the freedom pedestal into a maelstrom evoking the primordial chaos of Earth. Foursquare around the base flames of freedom rise in witness to the future."

This happens in New York City every night.

After we taste the fountain and feel the effects of spending time with it, let's ease down the sloping sidewalk of Amsterdam Avenue. About fifty yards on our right is the façade of the Cathedral of St. John the Divine. When you look at the façade as a whole, IT IS DIFFICULT TO KNOW WHETHER WE ARE WITNESSING A BUILDING STILL BEING BUILT **or one that is being DEMOLISHED.** Is it a cathedral on the rise or one going to ruins?

Walter Benjamin, a great cruiser, loved ruins and felt that walking through the ruins of a past civilization was the clearest tour of our souls that civilization could ever provide. To see useful buildings and holy places that meant something in the past and are now a remnant bereft of color and utterly useless is to see the arc of our own lives. There is so much in our lives that we currently take seriously and that means a great deal to us and that will eventually become **the ruins of *forgettability***.

The cathedral's two towers are not quite towers. Officially, the Cathedral of St. John the Divine is being built and not destroyed, although do not allow this announcement to interfere with your own interpretation of this cathedral's destiny. If it is partially built this means that part of its initial vision is in rubble.

Most people I have toured the cathedral with assumed that its unfinished state is a product of lack of funds rather than of lack of faith. I had to gently explain to them that St. John's current unfinishedness is more the influence of God than of finances.

This cathedral is sculpted by the great sculptor, God. God has crafted a Dadaist sculpture, which means that it is an art object that refuses to be just an object. It is not a cathedral that will be completed by architects and construction workers; this is a work of art that can only be completed by us.

The cathedral rings out with the message, "This world is one of God's experiments; he wants to see if we can love on our own." **This world is created by a God that has everything except our love. Jesus Christ** was a tour guide of love who gave a profound tour of the laws of love. He described a great party when he said, "Love others the way I have loved you."

As we walk up the staircase, which is uplifting and a challenge simultaneously, there may be artisans chiseling away at statuary that is being crafted right before our eyes.

The large bronze doors have sixty relief panels that depict

sixty highlights from the Old and New Testaments, sculpted by **Henry Wilson.** These panels are a long series of men on horses, men on their knees, men in agony, and men in the light of God. As I enter the cathedral, I am aware that Orthodox Judaism considers a Jew's entrance inside a church to be an automatic **sin.** I feel exuberant as I bipedal into sinfulness.

Through the front doors, we enter the **narthex.** This is a giant entrance hall designed to prepare you for prayer. **We are immediately greeted by the BOX OFFICE.** The space that surrounds us is immense. It is a Gothic exclamation covered in images of Christ and the feelings that lead to his wisdom. There is an entire world waiting for us on the other side of the box office.

The juxtaposition is larger than life, and as we pay admission—currently two dollars—we are illuminated with the truth that this cathedral believes it can only maintain itself through money rather than through the preeminence that it represents. It feels that it must impose mediocre human intercourse, the transaction, on visiting pilgrims at the end of their pilgrimage. It is an enormous comment about the world we currently live in that even an immense expression of God's power, a cathedral, has been wracked with such a lack of self-confidence.

If the Cathedral of St. John the Divine is feeling this much self-doubt, it is a wonder that any of us can get out of bed at all. Let this observation lead to yourselves thanking yourselves for having the courage to be alive.

The transaction greeting us in the narthex is the essential gesture of New York City's history. It is the most mediocre exchange of human feeling known to man. Here, we are being greeted with an exchange rather than a sharing. **(See also "Wall Street: The Story of What Happened to Our Intimacy.")**

All buildings give us opportunities to identify with them and when we enter the narthex, we are given our first opportunity to identify with a one-hundred-and-twenty-five-foot vaulted ceiling that stretches to the length of two football fields. In the distance, we have a chance to identify with the granite columns around the choir that weigh one hundred and thirty tons apiece and soar fifty-five feet high.

On the south end of the narthex, the first two window bays set the tone immediately. ***THE STAINED-GLASS WINDOWS ARE SHAPED LIKE ANGEL'S WINGS.*** The first bay tells the story of Saint Hubert. The stained glass in the second bay celebrates sports. One window meticulously observes St. Hubert's lineage while the window next to it portrays ancient-looking Christians playing soccer, basketball, and tennis. All of these events are equated as mystical events worthy of being subject matter for a cathedral's stained glass, all created by God's infinite expression.

As we enter the **nave** and face the altar for the first time, let us try to understand God in the framework of partying (because anything can be understood through the framework of **partying**). Partying means the state where everyone's happiness depends on everyone else's happiness, a space where a group of souls pursue exhilaration together and utilize their togetherness to get to exhilarated. A great party is one where each individual achieves a holiness entirely his or her own, and everyone is entertaining, and so everyone is entertained. *Jesus Christ was good at parties. He knew how to exhibit thrill and share it with others.* ***This is why they crucified him.***

Along the walls of the nave there are tapestries displaying highlights from Christ's career as a tour guide. There are images of him bringing men to the top of mountains to give them new perspectives, turning large lakes into dance floors as he dances on top of the waves, and there are several portrayals of moments of clarity being shared between him and others who seek the party that never ends. These tapestries are images that were originally painted by Raphael and then sampled here by seventeenth-century thread-wielding hip-hop masters.

In fact, I would say that the cathedral is a giant originality fashioned for the purpose of ringing out the message of participation and how originality springs from the loins of participating in each other's lives. All the unlikely decorations inside, including a set of menorahs in the choir, portrayals of Buddha, and all the unique connections the holy place has made with the surrounding neighborhood of vast varieties of ethnicities are originalities that are singing to God with new songs.

The cathedral is in a perpetual state of ascension and demoliton because we are. We are all here together with St. John attempting to find a new way to believe in God. ***This place recommends ORIGINAL and FUN WAYS to GOD.***

The nave has the enormity and austerity of any Gothic cathedral, but the recent art installations added by the living population inside this ancient and symbolic space are friendly and colorful. An intimacy is being promoted between us as God surrounds us with omniscient power and stone.

The exhibition of faith is participation in the world. It is not a matter of doing "good works" as much as it is about fashioning "good reality" that is theatrical and, most important, entertaining. There is not actually **"good"** or **"evil"** in the world, as much as there is **"good theater"** and **"bad theater."**

The floor is an original mixture of eight different marbles gathered from around the world. At times gray, at times blue, the floor is so smooth and dimly lit that it has the look of a dance floor or a fashion runway. Black medallions with layered gold leaf are embedded in the floor at great distances from each other. Each medallion is dedicated to a place of pilgrimage. A place of pilgrimage is a place where an entire population comes and goes in the name of God. New York City is one of these places.

The fifth window bay on the north side of the nave, the side to our right when facing the altar, is the **Medical Bay.** At the center of the bay is an altar of solid backing, also known as a reredos. This reredos is made of English oak and it shows us what it should look like when a doctor is successfully healing himself through healing other people.

A gray flag sprinkled with rainbow colors emblazoned "**The AIDS Memorial**" sits next to the medical altar. There are no visualizations or metaphors in the memorial that stir emotions, and so we must feel the pain of this plague in the spelling of the word. ***The AIDS plague has killed some of the funnest people among us. The plague's greatest impact, however, has been a death blow to the ramparts of our eroticism.***

The necessary dialogue involved in a traditional "father-son" or "mother-daughter" chat about sex today is no longer just about the mating rituals of birds and bees. It is, instead, an early introduction to mortality and the ultimate meta-irony the human population has always faced—the equating of sex and death. The damage this has done to our ability to let loose at parties is immeasurable. **Revolutions begin when people go without food. *Armageddons and Judgment Days begin when people go without sex.***

Midway through the nave, on the northern wall, is a bay that has become an aquarium. Exotic fish swim in God's name and celebrate being alive with the rest of the pilgrims who have come here for that purpose. St. John the Divine is famous for its celebration of **St. Francis of Assisi Day**, when an incredible caravan of animals, usually led by an elephant, comes into the cathedral for an annual blessing in mid-October.

The **choir** is the central platform sitting directly under the tiled dome at the end of the nave. On the way to the choir, we pass through the cathedral's **crossing.** This is the most unfinished piece of the cathedral's interior and its naked concrete is a reminder that the ceiling above us is made of steel. Officially, a cathedral is a building made of stone. The walls of the Cathedral of St. John the Divine are made of stone, but the roof is made of steel. The roof is not considered part of the cathedral. No cathedral should ever be obligated to have a roof. **It is an obstacle to reaching God.** The ingredient of steel high above our heads, however, is a specific New York City choice. Many cathedrals of the past had roofs fashioned out of lead sheets supported by heavy timber. It is certainly reasonable to pray in this modern metropolis under a halo of steel. When one cruises New York, it is easy to believe that steel is a primary ingredient of Heaven's gates.

Skirting the immense choir are eight enormous granite columns that form a hallway which branches off into seven chapels known as the **Chapels of Tongues.** *ST. COLUMBA'S CHAPEL, DEDICATED TO ALL THOSE OF CELTIC DESCENT, EXHIBITS INFLUENTIAL FIGURES FROM THE HISTORY OF THE ENGLISH CHURCH PILED UP ON TOP OF EACH OTHER ALONG THE OPENING ARCHWAY, VOGUEING.* The **St. James Chapel** is dedicated to the patron saint of Spain. At the time it was built, in 1916, there was no way of knowing that the cathedral would be surrounded by a Spanish-speaking population, and yet someone somehow knew. The St. James Chapel was dedicated to those of Spanish descent and they answered the beckoning. They are a population that has traversed great distances and great dismays to be here today.

In the **St. Saviour Chapel** behind the choir, sits the last work of the artist **Keith Haring.** Haring was an acclaimed graffiti artist who approached graffiti the way Renaissance painters approached painting on a canvas. Haring inhereted from the Renaissance a defiance of the museums, not of the cathedrals. Art that does not fit into collections but is founded on life. Just like the Dadaist sculptor of this building, Haring creates art meant to be participated in and lived with. The ongoing attempt in the history of art to reconcile art and life is an example of how much fun it can be to have faith in humanity. Haring's last work, currently on display, was conceived right after he was diagnosed with AIDS and completed just before his death.

The **Baptistry**, designed by **Frank Cleveland**, is a Gothic mix of French, Spanish, and Italian characteristics. It was given by the Stuyvesant family—the descendants of Peter Stuyvesant, infamous Dutch administrator of Nieuw Amsterdam. There are references to early New York history, including a sculpture of the one-legged Stuyvesant, throughout the baptistry. Christ writhes on a crucifix hanging on the western wall in front of a colorful and chaotic painted backdrop. It is a resurgence of the Peace Fountain's flowing portrayal of "the primordial chaos of Earth." This is one of the few landmarks in the city that knows about New York's HOLINESS, and has found it through the adoration of the city's CHAOS.

Standing inside the choir, we are dwarfed by the **rotunda** high above. Suddenly, you should feel so small. For the rest of our lives, everything will seem more enormous than before because we now know what it is to feel this small. From here, we have a dynamic view of the largest stained-glass window in the cathedral, the **rose window**, high up on the western wall. The blossoming rose hovering high above all these images of Christ's career turns the resurrection into a logical epilogue to a party where people showed up to be shared.

Now I am standing at the great altar of this cathedral party, surrounded by its immense organ, and I am thinking of Jesus Christ and the greatest rock 'n' roll concerts I have been to, all at once. I am praying. **What am I praying for? For this party to get better.**

Christ said, "Love others as I have loved you." We have had two thousand years to learn this simple lesson, and we have built many immense cathedrals in the name of learning it, yet we're still missing the essence of it. **In a moment, this entire place is reduced in my eyes, and now it seems to me an immense kindergarten in the eternal school of partying.**

We Do Not Fear Death as Much as We Fear Immortality: Madison Square Park

The dust of many crumbled cities settles over us like a forgetful doze, but we are older than those cities.

—Rumi

The number one cause of death is life.

—Lars Vegas

Armageddon knows us all by the same name!
I've only seen death in this life
on the commuter train, on the commuter train...

—Bard Omar

Standing beside my grandfather as he drew his last breath, my reaction as that very last breath soars toward the ceiling was to ask the following, "Where the hell are you going?" I am filled with curiousity rather than lamentation and in that mystical moment, I realize **the word DEATH IS less a WORD and more a CONNOTATION.** The connotation, *death,* is a desperate implication that is trying to imply that we know what happens when the body expires.

Truthfully, the only death I am sure I have seen is the one that occurs when **sullenness** comes calling. **DEATH is life taking itself too seriously.**

A person seeing the big picture does not die, he unites; does not get destroyed, but creates space for new birth. Malthus observed this and was persecuted by those frightened by the simple observation.

Havoc is happening every time we try to know the unknowable. This is why I start each of my days with the mantra, "**I don't know.**" When you trace the mechanical workings of our denial, you will see that the things that terrify us most are never mentioned. When you trace carefully the fine-tuned dance steps of our denying lifestyle, you can clearly see that all of our philosophizing and open talking about the fear of death is a ruse. What we really fear is immortality.

The reason everybody is so obsessed with solutions and proven equations, punctuation, and certainty is because everybody wants to know where the end is. An end is the easiest thing to grasp.

Therefore, **Madison Square Park** and every neighborhood ever built is actually an innovative way to create ruins. All buildings are pyramids, hysterical episodes constructed by the parts of us that want to believe there is an end. A population has built a population of buildings, their mark on this world, a kind of hoping that they will never have to return to a world built of their past accomplishments and disgraces.

Madison Square Park—once this city's largest graveyard—has transformed itself into a business center and a place to be seen. **Transformation** is life, and the intensity of a city's transformations is directly related to its greatness. **Today the gravestones have become**

SKYSCRAPERS. This is a cemetery filled with life that is GAINING ALTITUDE BEFORE OUR VERY EYES.

Welcome to Madison Square Park!

WE BEGIN AT 26TH STREET AND MADISON AVENUE, WHICH IS THE NORTHEAST CORNER OF THE PARK:

The **New York Life Insurance Company Building** stands just north of Madison Square's northeast corner at **Madison Avenue** between **26th and 27th Streets.** Designed by **Cass Gilbert** and completed in 1928, it is the building capped with an exclamation point in the form of a gold pyramid. It shines brightly on a sunny day, is a subdued remnant of a vaguely referred to past glory on cloudy days, and each night is one of the brightest spectacles of the New York skyline.

THE PYRAMID IS AN ANCIENT ARCHITECTURAL TACTIC used by tribes as varied and spread out as the Mayans and the Egyptians. The Mayans and the Egyptians existed in completely different worlds, but they shared an essential characteristic—original thinking. Both populations used the pyramid to revere the unknown and to express infinity.

This New York Life Insurance Company pyramid feels more like an architectural reference than a dedication to the idea of forever.

If there is a God being prayed to here, it is the GOD OF GOOD INVESTMENTS.

An insurance company succeeds by pretending that there is such a thing as *death*. To be a citizen of this society, you must believe that you need insurance, which is to say, to be a citizen of this society you must believe you are going to die; therefore, many of those who are having trouble fitting into the society are people too imbued with the knowledge of their own infinity.

Immortality, perhaps our greatest probability and responsibility whose very plausibility causes us to run crazily from all possibility, would view ***the New York Life Insurance Company and its building as the sad attempt of immortal beings trying to convince themselves that their objects last longer than they do.*** The fact of the matter is plain: We are older than time and space.

To recognize the magnitude of **karma**—the laws of time and space—is to know how much easier it is to become immortal through action and deed than it is to spend your life pretending to be immortal instead of spending your life becoming immortal.

The New York Life Insurance Company pyramid is a gravestone-temple built by atheists. **MODERN MAN'S ATHEISM is not a disbelief in the possibility of God. Modern man needs the IDEA OF GOD. When he says he DOES NOT BELIEVE IN GOD what he is really saying is that he wants to REPLACE GOD**. God, after all, is just another job at the top of a hierarchy. God is a job modern man thinks he can do better.

Cross **26th Street and Madison Avenue** and enter the limestone edifice of the New York Life Insurance Company Building. Waltz into the lobby and breathe in the imperialism of daydreaming Romans. This building was built by a superpower not quite born. Hang with the enormous hanging lanterns, and stand with the even larger ornate bronze doors that are the secular rebuttal to the baptistery doors of Florence.

On the **Park Avenue side of the lobby** is an entrance to the subway system complete with a grand staircase that is probably what Michelangelo would have thought of were he assigned to design a subway entrance.

Michelangelo once commented that all architecture is the recapitulation of the human body.

Just as we disappear in this bodily form but remain in people's thoughts, a destroyed building still has weight.

The **World Trade Center Towers** have an even more potent existence and impact on the human population as formless entities than they did when they had form. **(For more on the World Trade Center's current existence, refer to your own thoughts of it.)**

Stare into a candle for a full minute. Close your eyes. Can you still see the flame—bright, at times blinding—in your mind's eye? This exercise is a way to ***PRACTICE ETERNITY.*** It will sharpen your ability to feel the continuous influence of the **second Madison Square Garden** all around us.

This square block was the site of Stanford White's **Madison Square Garden.** The hyperbolic admixtured of High Spanish Renaissance and American sports arena was created in 1890 and destroyed in 1925. From Mother City's perspective, the Madison Square Garden that is a functioning High Spanish Renaissance structure and the Madison Square Garden that is a pile of rubble are the same. **(For more on Stanford White, see "A Tour Of Washington Square Park and My Heart: Fear Is Joy Paralyzed.")**

Every time a profiteer levels a beautiful building in the name of *progress*, he is an inadvertent secret operative of this city-teacher's brave mission to explain to us who we are. The city's discourse on the topic of creation and destruction is an echo of the universe's discourse on creation and destruction. The **city** and the **universe** have a ***lot in common.***

Madison Square Garden's tower, influenced by a tower in Seville's central square, was crowned by a nude **Diana**. The mounting of this statue was a major controversy in 1890. The public display of nudity was considered by many to be the beginning of society's downfall.

The Victorian era's repressed sexuality arose from the deeper depravity of **self-censorship. (For more on self-censorship, refer to "A Tour of Ladies Mile: Women Are Life.")**

Self-censorship is, most of all, a censorship of our possibilities. Our age is just as afraid of our possibilities as the Victorians were. At the end of the nineteenth century, society feared exploration of our bodily possibilities. At the end of the twentieth century, society fears the exploration of our mind's possibilities. In both epochs, exploration is the enemy.

The only thing I am opposed to in this life is becoming enslaved to a singular point of view. *Whenever I am dogmatic, I know I am having a crisis.* When I stood over my grandfather's last breath, I felt curiosity before I felt lamentation, I realized that his final lesson for me was that **suffocation**, if nothing else, is the birth of a new point of view.

Perspective is the key to enjoying life and executing meaningful **explorations.**

Today, Diana, the statue, can be viewed up close, lewdly and personally at the **Philadelphia Art Museum.**

The tall, black monolith building is the **Merchandise Mart Bank.** It looks a great deal like the monolith in the film *2001.* Those who have seen that film are aware of the significant implications of having an enormous black monolith that has silently landed in the middle of New York City.

In the film *2001,* the monolith is there the first day that Australopithecus realizes that sticks and stones can be used as weapons, and the monolith is in space when man first understands how much he has in common with the stars. The monolith is now here, on Madison Square Park, silent and waiting for the next revolution in our evolution. **(For more about our evolution, see "The Midtown Rush Hour Tour.")**

The **Leonard Jerome House**, built in 1859 in the heart of this graveyard's opulence, was apparently one of the most spectacular single-family residences of New York architectural history and was destroyed to make way for this black monolith. Leonard Jerome's daughter was named **Jennie Jerome**. Jennie moved to England, eventually married Lord Randolph Churchill, and went on to become **Sir Winston Churchill's** mother.

Next door to the monolith is the **Appellate Division Court of New York.** It is a limestone menace concocted by **James Brown Lord**, and completed in 1900. The façade is insane with its feelings of self-importance and the fact that *justice*—the most violent myth of civilization's current reign—is peddled inside daily. *There are so many wondrous FLAVORS OF REALITY.* **Judgment takes the taste out of all of them.** Judgment takes the fun out of almost anything.

The sixteen statues that line the Appellate Court building's cornice are all great figures in law. There are plush portraits of **Solon**, **Moses**, **Confucius**, and **Alfred the Great**. But there are no statues of the **Marquis de Sade,** who said, "Be honest, be fair; tolerate crime," or of **Robespierre**, democracy's greatest innovator, who once said, "Justice is unreachable. We persecute enemies of the state!"

Right across the street from the Appellate Division Court building is a playground—compare and contrast.

The statues are staring wisely at the **Metropolitan Insurance Company Building**, which is seated across the street, the mountain of granite with severe angles that is obviously a building from the world of Batman comic books. Gotham City is a city some of us dwell in more than others. This building is a piece of that imagined city gaining stony flesh.

The city is eternity out for a stroll. It is also, at all times of day, in all variances of illumination, a grave. We, the city's population, are remnants of many lost ages together experiencing a transition that is astrological and immense, while living in a grave filled with sexy dames and great restaurants. **This *is* a comic book.**

The clock tower on the corner that so effectively punctuates the discombobulated skyline of Madison Square Park's east side is also part of the **Metropolitan Insurance Company Building**, designed by **Napolean Le Brun** and completed in 1909. This tower is having a dialogue with the famous clock tower of San Marco Square in Venice, Italy. It was the tallest building in the world once upon a time. According to legend, the elderly **Mr. Woolworth**, king of the five-and-dime stores, marched out of the lobby of this building insane with rage one afternoon. He had been rejected by the Metropolitan Insurance Company when he applied for a policy. He was too old. He cried out for revenge and with his quivering, dying voice he proclaimed the beginning of his new project—a building with his name on it that would be even taller than the Metropolitan Insurance Company's building.

The **Woolworth Building** was erected by 1913 and was instantly the tallest building in the world. The lobby is, to this day, one of the most grandiose lobbies in New York City and the whole place takes on the aura of a cathedral with an attitude problem. Today thousands of people work arduously in the Woolworth Building, housed in WALLS ERECTED BY THE MOTIONS OF A MAN CONVINCED OF HIS MORTALITY, yet striving for I M M O R T A L I T Y. The people working within those walls are actively doing the same. Right now, the entire city is doing this as well.

When **Buddha**—the greatest tourist of all time—returned from a tour of all his past lives his friends asked him how many lives he had lived before this one. He answered, "I cannot give you an exact number, but put it this way . . . the amount of tears I've cried through all the lives I've led could fill an ocean."

The statue of **Roscoe Conkling**, just inside the **southeast**

corner of the park, is also the ongoing event of Roscoe Conkling being *immortalized.* Conkling is now half monument, half man. He was a lawyer and a retired senator when he walked out of his office early one evening and into the giant blizzard of March 12, 1888. The statue is standing on the spot where, disoriented by the tremendous storm, he collapsed. As a monument, he is the personification of ineptitude in the realm of reading weather. As a man, he represents frailty.

Immortality is a part of our every day. When immortality interacts with language *exaggerations* take place. An exaggeration is not an exaggeration. ***Your will to exaggerate is your will to see things as an immortal might.*** When Peter screamed wolf, when Natasha-at-Times-Simone told me I was a great lover, when a woman tells a man she is fairly unconcerned with having children, all of these are expressions emanating from someone's moment of feeling immortal. This is why people are so courageous when it comes time to exaggerate in their résumés, but lose that courage when it comes to living their lives. **It is easier to admit our IMMORTALITY on paper than to the world.**

Facing Roscoe Conkling from the north side of Madison Square Park is a statue of the famous admiral **David Farragut.** The statue was sculpted by **Augustus Saint-Gaudens** and the base was crafted by **Stanford White.** Note the dolphins swimming on the surface of the pedestal and the wind, Mother Nature's embrace, blowing Farragut's frame into infamy. Farragut is buried in the Trinity Church's graveyard on Wall Street. (**For more about Trinity Church's graveyard, refer to "Wall Street: The Story of What Happened to Our Intimacy."**)

He led the Union navy to victories at New Orleans and Mobile Bay, which contributed to the Union's complete control of the Mississippi River and broke the Confederacy's back in the

American Civil War. **Farragut's famous last words, "*Damn the torpedoes! Full speed ahead!*" is a mantra for cruisers everywhere.**

I recommend visiting the statue of **Peter Cooper** which sits in front of the southern side of **Cooper-Hewitt (on Third Avenue and Saint Marks Place in the East Village)**, the monumental building and school constructed by Peter Cooper. That statue and its base are also the collaboration between White and Saint-Gaudens, but at a much later period in their lives, long after their friendship had broken apart and their egos had soared beyond control. The antithesis of this Farragut piece, the Cooper statue is not even as big as the base of the earlier work. Comparing and contrasting these two statues provides a breathtaking view of a friendship's harmony and dissonance.

On the southwest corner of the park is the statue of **William Seward**, secretary of state under **President Abraham Lincoln.** Seward was notably a short man and you can see that the limbs of his statue here are elongated and enormous. There are many who believe that this was originally a statue of a much taller man, namely **President Abraham Lincoln.**

According to legend (a rumor sanctified after being retold so many times) the sculptor's commission for an Abraham Lincoln statue fell through while he was crafting the piece. So, at the last moment, he chipped Lincoln's face off and replaced it with William Seward's countenance.

One man's economic motivations have played havoc with another man's portrayal. In New York terminology this statue is called a ***good business decision.*** In human terms, a man's life is being celebrated nonchalantly, even accidentally.

This statue is a monument and parody, all at once.

Seward was mocked when he decided to purchase Alaska. The American press called Alaska "Seward's Follies" or "Seward's Icebox." Seward's venture is the second most important land acquisition in American history, second only to the **Louisiana Purchase.** It has made many an American president horny.

In the years leading to the Civil War, Seward made several brave attempts to provoke war with foreign nations with the hope of refocusing the North and the South so their belligerence could be pointed outward, toward a foreign enemy.

Today the statue is green, as if to remind us that Seward is currently much more involved with the soil than with American history. Seward is now involved with a much larger, more incomprehensible process than anything so trivial as being a Cabinet member under Lincoln. His mother undoubtedly reprimanded him for getting dirt all over himself. This is too bad. After all, he was merely animated ashes on the verge of returning to sedentary ashes. When we sweep up dust in our living room we are sweeping up our own flesh. It's an almost-funny situation. **DOOM** *is an almost-funny feeling happening in the middle of an almost-unbearable situation.*

Doom is the comedic punch line to eternity because in our worst moment the only unbearable thought is the thought that this never ends. **Doom** is whenever we think we are at the end of something only to realize this ending is actually just a beginning. If they ever do find an end to the universe they will also find laughter.

Directly across **23rd Street** is a building that is custom-made for the triangulated confluence of Fifth Avenue and Broadway. It is called the **Flatiron Building.** Constructed in 1902, the building's awkwardness is also its precision. The Flatiron Building is here to prove that awkwardness is *beautiful,* and is a part of striving toward perfection.

Awkwardness is the electricity of living; you know something is really going on when you feel awkward. (**For more about this intersection, see "Broadway the Renegade."**)

According to legend, the famous American idiom *23 skiddoo* was originally a reporter's description of a daily event taking place on the construction site of the Flatiron Building.

A traffic cop would come each day to break up ***a phalanx of salivating construction men*** who would congregate at the apex of the new building's triangular base in order to watch the sudden gusts of wind blow women's skirts and dresses into the air. The wind's intensity had increased due to the new channel formed by the Flatiron's façade and the other side of Fifth Avenue.

This anecdote was a daily theater piece produced by the great city-dramatist. The women's skirts blown into the air represent limitless possibility. The men's reactions represent themselves feeling the limitless possibilities. The policeman's breaking up of the crowd is how society reacts to people feeling the limitless possibilities.

The word l i m i t l e s s is a *way of life*. It is a declaration of war against limitations. To take up arms in the name of limitlessness is to go where the unimaginable must go and it is to realize that security is a fantasy in this life and balance is a cop-out. Once you get a glimpse of how great the world is, once you taste the limitless possibilities all around you, there is no going back.

One of the oldest **lampposts** still standing on **Fifth Avenue** is across the street from the Flatiron's bow. This lamppost has witnessed the entire unraveling of this neighborhood and stood tall here when this was the most fashionable place to be seen, when Fifth Avenue was more a fashion runway than it was a street. This lamppost has illuminated faces looking and being looked at for a century. It is a monument, an eternal light, dedicated to all you voyeurs out there, and also to the voyeurs who built the Flatiron Building. The life of a voyeur is always a precarious one. **Be brave!**

Across the street, at the southwest corner of **23rd Street and**

Fifth Avenue, is **Henry Janeway Hardenbergh's Western Union Building.** Hardenburgh also designed the Plaza Hotel and the Dakota apartment building. Moments of Western Union's day are portrayed in meticulous engraved motifs along the cornice line of the red façade.

Across the street, on the **northwest corner of 23rd and Fifth**, is the **Toy Center Building**, completed in 1909. This building is an exact replica of the building that stood on this plot of land just before it. The father of this toy center was the old **Fifth Avenue Hotel**, completed in 1859. One of the most prestigious hotels of American history, the Fifth Avenue Hotel's bar was called the **Amen Corner** because its corner booths were famous locations for intrigue, the hatching of conspiracies, and the swinging of presidential elections. This was where Theodore Roosevelt won his first election.

The Toy Center Building and the Fifth Avenue Hotel are identical twins born fifty years apart. With this plot of ground, the city has crafted a story where a sacred alcove for influential Americans has become a center for the production and sale of toys, which makes sense if you are God or Mother City. Architecturally, the two events are represented identically. It is here that the city illustrates that **CHOOSING POLITICAL LEADERS AND CHOOSING WHICH TOYS WE LIKE TO PLAY WITH ARE BOTH CHOICES WE MAKE IN THE NAME OF ENTERTAINMENT.**

The **Eternal Light Monument** is the star shining at the top of the gigantic white flagpole that honors American soldiers who were killed in World War One. War is a creative way to go about dying. **WAR IS THE ACT of having a point of view.** War is dwelling within every proselytization for peace. **Self-destruction** is the utilization of the fear of immortality.

Floating in the middle of the wide intersection, just south of **26th Street and Fifth Avenue**, is the grave of **General William J. Worth.** Erected in 1857, the obelisk, an ancient symbol for remembering, marks the burial site of General Worth, a warrior in the Seminole and Mexican Wars. The Texas city of Fort Worth is named after him. A list of famous battles fought under General Worth's auspices are chiseled into the granite shaft.

Remembering is a far more **psychotic** episode than forgetting. Remembering is also ***sexier*** than forgetting.

Heaven and Hell are both places ruled by impotency, but perhaps the difference between them is that one tries to remember and the other tries to forget. Although I can't remember which one is trying to remember and which one is trying to forget.

General Worth's monument sits at a fork in the road between Fifth Avenue and Broadway. Let's start walking up Broadway's vein as it moves northwest from here, destined to cause great dysfunction and congestion to the north. **(For more on Broadway's destiny, see "Broadway the Renegade.")**

Here Broadway is about to collide with Fifth Avenue. Today, this boulevard is a bustling business district run by Koreans, Indians, Arabs, Haitians, Africans, and Dominicans. Looking up Broadway one sees a long diagonal line of buildings that look like sunken ocean liners docked on the shores of some ethereal body of water. ***This is the famous Tin Pan Alley***. As the twentieth century was being born, a hotbed of musicians, composers, music studios, and musical invention could be found here.

After electricity was invented by **Thomas Edison** in **Newark, New Jersey**, the theater districts of the city would be entirely lit up at night. The theater districts were always on Broadway, and sections of it throughout the generations were particularly spotlit. This area we are standing on became known as the **Great White Way** as it was a path bathed in a light that was vivaciously illuminating the mundane.

Follow the way into your own **Great White Way.**

Walk up the old Great White Way as if it is your own personal Great White Way with the confident strut that comes from knowing that **survival** is a mediocre goal, most of all because it is dogmatic about the idea that there is an oblivion. This is another example of us trying to know what we cannot currently know, which is to say, this is another good example of how we torture ourselves. Worst of all, self-preservation requires a certain humorlessness in application. **HUMORLESSNESS is synonymous with the state of being *unevolved*.**

Madison Square Park is a moving seance and a complicated joke whose punch line is infinity. Here, the city-teacher is laughing at the notion of *surviving* because survivalism, such a prominent fiction among us, is a killer.

Walk into your divine light, the place where this treacherous tour of ourselves leads, the way toward being aware of our own divinity and our never-ending light, not needing to make a big deal out of it.

This is the path that leads to our full realization that there is plenty of us to go around and that the love and energy that we possess is limitless and does not need to be handed out to others in teaspoons. This leads to the ability to just **hang out.**

IF YOU'VE TASTED YOUR **INFINITY** THEN YOU KNOW YOU HAVE **PLENTY OF TIME TO HANG OUT.**

This realization leads to becoming what society calls a **slacker**.

A Tour of Bloomingdale's: Suffering Is An Addicton to Self-Doubt . . . Maybe

Why were we born amongst mirrors?
—Federico García Lorca

WE BEGIN AT 59TH STREET AND LEXINGTON AVENUE—IN FRONT OF BLOOMINGDALE'S:

Shopping is a prayer to look good. Like your average prophet's life, a day of shopping is a monumental leap of faith and a hazardous shamanic journey through yearning. If a day of shopping or a prophet's prophecy is fully, gloriously realized, it results in a single moment of satisfaction not unlike that experienced after one sins successfully. The method that introspective people use to contemplate their way to perfection, the method of the builder building perfection, is the method of the shopper: **try it on**.

In a sense, what's really evolving here is our sense of style.

Heightened self-reflection does not only lead to enlightenment, it also leads to a huge wardrobe.

Bloomingdale's is a consumeristic Vatican, a holy destination, for a certain kind of pilgrimage made by a specific type of pilgrim. I have personally met thousands of souls who traversed half the Earth's terrain for the opportunity to visit Bloomingdale's. I have spent a day there with a caravan of forty Turkish women fresh from the ancient air of Istanbul. We shared no common language, no common rituals or traditions, yet the mere utterance of the word "Bloomingdale's" incited instant identification between us.

Bloomingdale's is a rare opportunity to investigate our sociology while passing in front of mirrors.

In the opening vestibule, we are faced with watches and women gesturing for us to come closer. **Louis Vuitton luggage** is off to our right, and down a short staircase there is the entrance to a cave in the basement called **The Men's Store.**

On the other side the vestibule there is a staircase we must ascend to enter the main lobby. With each step, one can feel the energy emanating from this famous endless series of counters. ***Instantly, we are surrounded by a form of capitalism that requires a gyration of human bodies similar to the dance one witnesses on the floor of the Stock Exchange.***

The specific gestures of this dance are different from the one on Wall Street, but the purpose, and therefore the dance steps, are similar. (**For more about the Stock Exchange, see "Wall Street: The Story of What Happened to Our Intimacy."**)

Stand among the **perfume counters**. You are wearing all the fragrances at once.

The name "Bloomingdale's" is a permutation of the original Dutch term "Bloemendaal," which means "vale of flowers." The original Bloemendaal is a town in the Netherlands. In New York City, the permutation "Bloomingdale" has been applied to the road that was prenatal Broadway in 1703, to the first insane asylum of the metropolis in 1821, and also to a dry goods store that opened in April 1872.

Vanity has been the prime mover in every manifestation of "Bloomingdale's" in New York history, but the department store presents the most obvious instance.

Vanity is self-appraisal addicted to **self-doubt.** *It is the invention of a person we can never be,* placing ourselves on a shelf impossibly out of reach along with the deodorant. Our vanity is a false illusion that our ancestors have preserved from generation to generation.

Vanity invented history so that we would pay top dollar for **facial lotions** that make us look like ourselves as we imagine we could be.

Find the busiest counter in your vicinity and stand within the business.

This version of Bloomingdale's before us is also a symbol of the Upper East Side's expansion. **Lyman and Joseph Bloomingdale** opened "the great East Side bazaar" with a first-day sales total of $3.68. The store would grow with the construction of the Third Avenue elevated train, completed in 1879, and by 1927, Bloomingdale's department store filled the square block it currently occupies between Lexington and Third Avenues.

Mass consumerism is the kind of capitalism that makes New York City seem exciting to people who live in mainland China. Mass consumerism is classlessness in the name of profit and it means that public emporiums are open invitations to anyone who wishes to spend money. The transcendence of class distinctions is simulated for the sake of sales. In the world of Bloomingdale's, a good citizen is one who knows where everything is. A good citizen knows where the discounts are.

Bloomingdale's and mass consumerism are both made possible by the anti-Cruise's doomsday device, also known as **com-**

mon sense. The brain's propaganda is the secret computer God of this Star Trek adventure. The Bloomingdale's moments when people are successfully feeling beautiful are not moments involving common sense, as the management might have you believe, and they are not any other manifestation of the brain's hysteria. Those penultimate and rare moments when we feel beautiful in Bloomingdale's are manufactured by our hearts.

Stretch like lycra through the skin-treatment centers of the **Estée Lauder Spa** and then go upstairs to the wilderness of **intimate apparel** and see if you can find intimacy there. Among all these hanging bras, the undergarment that is the most sensational meeting of rationality and irrationality known to man, let us consider what our common sense is doing to us.

Did you know that *common sense* was a term invented in the seventeenth century? For most of man's history it went unnamed.

Common sense is the department store of the mind.

Let's freely roam the arcade of counters and take in the imagery and the pulse of this place. To walk through hanging nylon stockings into a coliseum of panties resulting in a lineup of see-through blouses is to walk through a woman's body without touching her. We are standing in an enormous womanly body but we know nothing about her and she has no identity. She has been departmentalized, and so we cannot feel her and she cannot be felt.

Women figure here at Bloomingdale's to exhibit how mysterious it is to be a human being.

Originally, before civilization, men did not know that they, themselves, had anything to do with procreation. The women were just getting pregnant and the process was a mystical ocean to be revered. As I write these words, most men have allowed **biology**—the scientific excuse for lethargy—to convince them that a woman's fertility is explainable through diagrams. ***The***

lackluster attitude toward the miracle of birth is what leads to bad rock 'n' roll.

Bloomingdale's is a temple dedicated to *decay*, housing rituals of simulated self-adornment. The seriousness we feel in Bloomingdale's is so intense because this is how seriously we take our bodies. To depend on our bodies for happiness is to be driving a car off a cliff and staying in the car the entire time. One of the few things that is inevitable: the decrepitude of our bodies. Bloomingdale's is also a kindergarten guiding many by creating fantastic styles that are unwearable for the average person; it is a kindergarten in the school of finding enjoyment and pleasure outside the ramparts of the body. **Joy** is the first outer-body experience.

Stand next to a table of folded shirts or sweaters. The table begins each day in a pristine state, folded neatly into organized piles. By the end of the day, the shirts and sweaters have been tried on and discarded many times and the entire table is in disarray. Human touch, as usual, caused this chaos. *We ARE the shirts and sweaters.* Our need for human touch, as well as the shirts and sweaters, leads to absolute chaos in all our lives. This table of folded and unfolded garments and New York City are both chaotic because they have both been touched by human beings.

Bloomingdale's is a forest in the same way that the forest in Shakespeare's *A Midsummer Night's Dream* is a forest. They are both forests filled with love potions meant to make us into the perfect beings whom the people we idolize love. They are both forests filled with young lovers who are trying to escape the laws that keep them apart. ***Shakespeare, a great tour guide, shows us that wherever the love potion goes, chaos follows. Love is being enamored of each other's chaos.***

Take a moment with your reflection in a mirror. I never like to pass up an opportunity for self-reflection. We are currently the only animals on the planet equipped with this special ability to stare down ourselves. Bloomingdale's would not be possible if we could not do this.

Our **naïveté** is the part of ourselves that is still astonished after the first time we look into a mirror. If there is one part of us that will save the world it will be our *brave naïveté.*

Civilization will end here, in front of a mirror at Bloomingdale's, when a woman stares into it and has a moment of true satisfaction with what she sees, questions her satisfaction, and then **remains satisfied.**

A Tour of Ladies Mile: Women Are Life

Women are the Gods, women are life . . .
be ever among women in thought.
—Buddha

A woman can sexually receive her man for as long as she pleases . . . a man's love making is limited to the amount of energy he has to keep his erection . . . this sexual imbalance is the primary reason men have sought physical, financial, political, intellectual, and religious advantage over woman.
—Mantak Chia

Everything in my life has become dresses.
—Christian Dior

There is nothing disdained more than introspection. The fear of **self-awareness** is the fear of facing life directly. Every society is a fortification built to protect us from facing life directly. Every nation has experienced the oblivion that comes from obliviousness.

I believe all men are terrified of women and the best of them are the ones who can admit it. Many of the revelations that occur in this dialogue with the Ladies Mile historic district are revelations that no heterosexual man should have to face.

To all men everywhere, I am sorry.

Ladies Mile is an absurd vision of paradise manufactured by ***a whimpering society,*** desperate to disprove the omnipotence of female sex. The fact that women can go all night and a man is fortunate to last fifteen minutes is the real reason Ladies Mile is a historic landmark district today.

In the middle of the nineteenth century, the invention of the department store brought societal revolution. Ladies Mile was the major shopping district of turn-of-the-century New York City, where the department store and its effect on the world came to full fruition.

Before the onset of the department store, it had been a conformist understanding among the upper classes of New York society that a woman should not be seen alone on the streets of the city. The department store is the first place, along with the Broadway matinee, where women could be viewed publicly by themselves, bereft of male escort. Among departmentalizations of her anatomy, a woman is given an afternoon of autonomous, public gregariousness with one stipulation: she commits herself to being a doll. This is society's prison-house paradise for women.

Therefore, the department store is an X ray of society's view of women's paradise.

The department store is also an excellent place to view capitalism's need to understand human beings vaguely. To be profitable, the department store must treat women more as assemblages than as goddesses.

Categorization destroys mystery and this is why the department store is in departments. The department store is the apotheosis of society's desecration of awe as it pertains to the mystery that is woman.

Women are emissaries of mystery showing us, on a daily basis, how mysterious it can be to be a human being.

Women create the world and the men who created the department store, but not the mentality that goes along with it, which is man's attempt to explain, or at least contain, the mystery. **BY GIVING BIRTH TO MEN, WOMEN ARE THE CREATORS OF THE VERY ORGANIZATION THAT IS RUINING THEM.**

Society is something women are doing to themselves.

Welcome to "Ladies Mile!"

WE BEGIN AT 18TH STREET AND SIXTH AVENUE:

Today we stand on a new vision of "Ladies Mile." We find ourselves surrounded by an ongoing **shopping spree. A shopping spree is one of the most incredible events produced by Mother Nature.** This shopping spree is as sublime as the shark-feeding frenzies happening in the depths of the oceans right now. In this frenzy, mammals are discovering themselves in specific pieces of material matter. Then with cash, credit card, or personal check, they are appropriating that matter in the name of decorating their reality with it.

Cruising is the shopping spree where we are shopping for everything worthwhile in this existence, whatever that is at this moment. ***TOWELS and BLISS Are equally within reach in the middle of this incredible shopping spree.***

On the east side of **Sixth Avenue between 18th and 19th Streets**, the large "Big Store-City in Itself," with the outlandish terrace perched high atop its august façade, is the original **Sie-**

gal-Cooper's store. Today it is a **Bed, Bath and Beyond** and a **Filene's Basement.**

The Siegal-Cooper building looks like a dollhouse that has broken out of miniaturization, **a Barbie dream house that is now life-size but still housing dolls,** still dressing and undressing them, still filled with cookie plates and coffee mugs and the scenarios dreamed up by food-smudged girls playing alone.

The original department stores are illuminated views into society's ideas about what women want. The mother/whore paradigm—the original crime of civilization—is the assumption that women have two categories in our lives: mothers and whores. Once this assumption is in place, women are at all times being regarded as merely ongoing destinations for instant gratification and fleshy catalysts for a series of reflexes. The mother/whore paradigm and the Siegal-Cooper building are both the products of men who are unoriginal and who experience a one-dimensional understanding of women as food-delivering mechanisms.

Here is a dollhouse that believes it has a monopoly on an ideology known more commonly as **femininity.** *Femininity is an open, erotic affair with creation, with infinity expressing itself.* This is why women are chaos incarnate. Women are limitless beings currently contained by constructions that are necessarily depleting their joy; this is also called society.

When we walk inside the Siegal-Cooper store you can see two stores, both operating according to a specific understanding of **organization.** In fact, all the stores of Ladies Mile, whether expensive or cheap, share the same basic organizing principles—men's casual, women's intimate apparel, junior's outerwear, etc. All the stores of Ladies Mile, past and present, assume that organization is necessary for their operation.

Organization, whatever the ideology attached to it, is the anti-Cruise reflex to limit our limitlessness and a consecration device to foster enslavement to singular points of view. All organizations are meek echoes of the true organization—civilization. **Civilization is a tour guide who brings us to the edge of our graves.**

In Hindu mythology, **Shakti**—the goddess of female fertility and creativity—is buried in an open field by civilized man on the first day of civilization. **SOCIETY'S CONTINUALLY CRUELEST TACTIC HAS BEEN ITS SUCCESSFUL ATTEMPTS TO CONVINCE WOMEN THEY CAN MAKE PROGRESS IN IT.**

Feminism, just another organization that is as afraid of human possibility as any man, is an arrangement of prisoners trying to make their imprisonment more comfortable.

The world we live in is currently designed to keep women from being fully women, and so **to be a woman who is *really good at the game of society* is to be a woman *adept in the realm of her persecution*.**

The central feature on the main floor of the Siegal-Cooper store was a fountain made of marble that shot jets of water in different colors, and we are passing by the place where it once flowed as we descend into Filene's Basement. The water danced around a granite pedestal, which could be viewed through an open well-hole on the second floor. The fountain was a well-known place for the occasional rendezvous and midafternoon meeting between lovers. As we feel the spray of this once-fountain, once-here, and descend into Filene's Basement, let us consider the impact that the enormous combination of women and water has had on our lives.

Filene's Basement is literally in the basement, and as we descend into its fluorescent lighting we will be among racks and piles of discount clothing for women.

At the center of Hinduistic thinking, ***men do not exist and are known to be women dressed up in costume for the express purpose of entertaining women.*** This ancient thought is clearly true outside the **changing rooms** in Filene's Basement.

Follow the women toward the dressing rooms. Some of the women go back into the abbey of this cathedral and stay there. Other women reappear in new looks and parade themselves, awaiting a man's reaction.

This theatricality between the woman and her man is a dance between a puppet pulling the puppeteer who pulls the puppet for the reaction she wants. It is amazing to see how ***many of the women in Filene's Basement are masochists***, creating men who entertain them by being permanently unimpressed with them.

Upstairs, in Bed, Bath and Beyond, we enter a vast and enormous corridor of shelves and rotisseries. Sultans of the Ottoman Empire did not have this kind of selection.

When we exit the Siegal-Cooper building, step away from the enormous store so that we can see the entire façade. It is ornate above the second floor but not below the second floor.

The street we're standing on is Sixth Avenue. It is wide and straight, and back when Ladies Mile meant something, it supported an elevated train. The ground floors of these buildings lay in the shadows of this elevated railroad, and if a building was going to attract the attention of would-be consumers passing by on the train, the second floor had to be the part of the building that caught the eye of that vast, moving population.

All of these Sixth Avenue turn-of-the-century department stores have façades that are flamboyant only for the sake of elevated-train passengers. Like a man dancing on a dance floor to impress a woman, who stops dancing whenever she stops looking, these buildings are so imbued with agenda that they only feel the need for purposeful extravagance.

This is beauty as defined by a beauty pageant. This is beauty being utilized more than experienced. These buildings' goals are more alive than they are.

As we cross the street, take a moment to sense the lingering aura of **Bonwitt Teller**, a store that began here in 1895 and later moved up to Fifth Avenue and 13th Street. It's final location, on 57th Street and Fifth Avenue, was destroyed in the late 1970s after it had already been incorporated into the austere carnival called **Trump Tower.** Reputable in the exclusive circles of the city, Bonwitt Teller's original Ladies Mile building no longer exists, but its shattered faith in this world can still be felt in the air.

The **mall** has taken over modern America's terrain, which is to say, *COMFORT is more important to Americans than originality*. Bonwitt Teller's fine fabrics, sold to ostentatious and hardcore fetishists, have become obsolete. If Bonwitt's considered women to be ornaments, the ornaments it had in mind were plush pillowy canopy beds. If a suburban mall today considers women as ornaments, the ornament is a clean kitchen floor.

Edith Wharton, author of *The Age of Innocence,* was born at **14 West 23rd Street** in a small building that was once the James McCutcheon and Company store, known as *The Linen Store.* The store specialized in fine linen—tablecloths, napkins, doilies, and pillowcases. It was in this building that Wharton first felt insane.

Across the street from Siegal-Cooper is the original **B. Altman Store—The Palace of Trade.** The building was designed by D. and J. Jardine. Today, the store is called **Today's Man.**

Benjamin Altman specialized in fine silks, velvets, satins, sculpture, and ceramics. He was also a major art collector and donated a lofty possessiveness, and the booty of that possessiveness, to the Metropolitan Museum of Art.

Altman was a bachelor who sold high-quality fabric to

women to make dresses for themselves using the newly invented sewing machine. His delivery wagons were distinguished by their shiny maroon skin, rubber tires, and brass carriage lamps. He was a "considerate employer," shortening the generally accepted sixty four-hour work week for his laborers and supplying them with a subsidized cafeteria.

Walk inside Today's Man store and witness the opening panoramic view of the expansive room filled with the spirit of all that is debonair. As we peruse the store, note any manifestations of the assumption that women want to be integrated into society.

Among the blazers and other visions of masculinity around you, consider that only lethargic women could believe that economic well-being means independence. Only lethargic women could demand *equal rights.* Hang out with the man who checks the bags at the front of the store and wonder out loud, "Does a diva demand equality?" **A DIVA IS RECOGNIZED AS A DIVA BECAUSE SHE DEMANDS REVERENCE.** A diva is a woman who has acknowledged her Godhood. She has recognized that she is an emissary of the universe and the creator of all men.

There is usually a good sale on leather belts in Today's Man.

Across the street from the original B. Altman's is the red brick **Cammeyer's Shoe Store** of the late nineteenth century. This store raised the standards for shoes and the sale of shoes. Cammeyer's "standard of merit" slogan became synonymous with quality footwear and is now a mantra shared between a man and a woman when they are in the initial stages of dating. **Our judgments about who is a fitting mate for us and which shoes are right for us: decisions being made by the same parts of the brain.**

Cammeyer's moved uptown to 34th Street in 1917, yet another establishment following the affluent population of the city.

The fine Italian lines of this building present a quiet masculine presence among the other buildings around here, which offer different angles of the same wedding cake.

The masculinity unfolding on this corner is warning men today saying,

> Give up! Surrender! You can't win!
> Any man who currently thinks he has power over the women in his life is in great danger.

and

> The source of a woman's allure is within you!

and

> When we are trying to figure out how to deal with the women around us we are figuring out how to live!

New York City, the great city-teacher, has crafted this Ladies Mile and its story to remind us that **MEN and *women* are each other's greatest lessons.**

The former **Church of the Holy Communion** is across the street and is today the **Limelight**—the nightclub that was once a church. What were pews are now bars. Love in this realm is proven to be deformed. Love in this realm is missing one of its primary ingredients—courage. The loud music and the blaring lights are exciting theatrical devices that are obvious defensive measures mounted against the possibility for intimacy. The women, metaphysical beings driven insane by this limited existence within a human body, dance with men they themselves created for entertainment and purposes of distraction.

The **Hugh O'Neill Store** across the street from the Limelight is a Palladian invention that still has the name O' Neill running across the top of the building's façade. O'Neill's famous motto: "A sewing machine in every home." The sewing machine became a symbol for security and "making it" in America for the struggling immigrant family. After the initial disillusionment that came with the realization that the streets were not actually paved with gold came the immediate need to get a job as a tailor. The immigrant began by tailoring his clothes and in some instances went on to tailor the clothes of other people, until eventually he tailored himself, cutting himself down till he was a right and proper American.

Walk down to **14th Street** and take a left.

Fourteenth Street is the longest crosstown byway on Manhattan Island, measuring two and a half miles. Two blocks to the east of **Sixth Avenue and 14th Street** is **Union Square Park,** the Times Square of the city at the turn of the century. Fourteenth Street still has the air of a major artery, and its commerce is straight-on immigrant. The energetic selling occurring on 14th Street today is a ballistic situation ***recommended for any appreciators of* capitalism's *BEAUTY.*** Fourteenth Street is an ongoing athletic contest of heckling and bartering and screaming. My cousin Bruce told me that 14th Street is where he goes when he wants to rekindle his memories of chaotic Bombay. **(For more on Cousin Bruce, refer to "A Tour of Washington Square Park and My Heart: Fear Is Joy Paralyzed.")**

One block away is an intersection that currently houses a bank on the northwest corner, a gymnasium on the southwest corner, a Korean deli on the northeast corner, and a small coffee shop on the southeast corner. **Ferrand Léger**, the French cubist painter, would tell his personal confidantes that his favorite intersection in all of New York City was this one, **14th street and Fifth Avenue**. Leger even created an outdoor sculpture for this intersection entitled "Walking Flower," a multicolored, eight-foot strutting flower. (When the city displayed it several summers ago, they had to ask Mrs. Léger if they could do so on 57th Street and Park Avenue instead of 14th and Fifth.) Walk to this intersection that looks like an uninspired collection of simple urbania and attempt to stand in Fernard Léger's shoes. Find what Léger found here.

Between Fifth and Sixth Avenues, on the south side of the busy street, is **56 West 14th Street.** This tall, thin building is the original **Macy's Dry Goods Store.** You may be able to see the transluscent name of "Macy's" as it persists under a new coat of paint over the front door of the building. Notice the engraved faces floating on either side of the cornice. Are these faces ***eyeing us*** and the other passersby as ***prey,*** or are these faces *flabbergasted?* **You decide.**

Rowland Hussey Macy started three different dry goods stores when he first came inland at the end of his career as a whaler. The fourth version is now one of the largest department stores in the world and occupies an entire square block at 34th Street and Seventh Avenue.

The famous red-star logo of Macy's is a reproduction of the original red-star tattoo on the original Mr. Macy's forearm. The red star is actually one of the more well-known tattoos of Western civilization.

Macy was a hunter, a whaler. This means that **when he shared present tense with a WHALE he was more likely to harpoon it than to stand absorbed in wondrous awe as it swam by.**

The difference between these two reactions lies in the difference between *appreciating beauty* and *appropriating beauty.*

Ladies Mile is an ongoing opportunity to experience the difference between appreciating beauty and appropriating beauty.

The difference between being an appreciator and being an

appropriator lies within our own ability or inability to appreciate the beauty of ourselves.

Beauty is here to help us fall in love with ourselves.

The **flamboyant** are those who actually appreciate the beauty of themselves.

The **gaudy** are those who mimic this appreciation.

Falling in love with someone is to become alert to the Godhood of that someone. You are as riveted and elevated face-to-face with a lover as you would be face-to-face with a God; *TO FALL IN LOVE IS TO SEE THE DIVINE SPARK AND FEEL THE GOOEY ETERNITY OF ANOTHER'S BOUNDLESS LUSCIOUSNESS.*

From this lofty plateau, one can see the mother/whore paradigm is the centerfold in the history of man.

The Virgin Mary and Mary Magdalen had a great deal in common; they were both women who loved Jesus Christ. If there was anyone who saw how similar they really were it was probably Christ himself. Due to this misanthropic analysis of Christ's women, Natasha-Sometimes-Simone is a woman who is really two women, both jealous of each other.

Wasn't the French Revolution finally incited by Marie Antoinette and her fleshy lascivious liveliness? She was assassinated by the people long before she was brought to the guillotine when the population accused her of generally being a whore, which is to say, when Paris accused her of reveling in her sexuality instead of being their asexual matriarch. Marie Antoinette did not properly categorize herself. ***DEFYING*** THE RIGID CATEGORIZATION OF THE MOTHER/WHORE PARADIGM IS THE MOST DRASTIC ACTION A WOMAN CAN TAKE IN CIVILIZATION.

Due to the mother/whore paradigm, I spend a ton of money on nude massages and I still come off looking like a good citizen!

Due to the mother/whore paradigm, men and women have been convinced that there are only a couple of things they can be together, and only a couple of activities they can share together.

Why else would copulation so often be nothing more than two people coming together to feel alone?

Central Park: Mother Nature Is Cosmopolitan

New York City is as much a part of nature as honeycomb.
—Terrence McKenna

Take your concentrated focus off the ineptitude of your human parents and place it instead on your original mother—nature. For her love is omniscient and unconditional . . .
—Guruji, to his suffering disciples

Manhattan is an experiment in alchemical denial as it mixes with preferences called **Civilization.** Manhattan is a place where civilization—this perplexed chapter the human race is currently experiencing as it prepares itself to live—evicts the original mother.

Therefore, **Central Park.**

Twenty-seven thousand trees transplanted, ten and a half

million cartloads of topsoil imported, and over a hundred miles of drainage pipes laid. These are the basic ingredients of Central Park. In the end, they say they used twice as much gunpowder to build Central Park as was used in the Battle of Gettysburg. Fifty-three thousand men died at Gettysburg.

There is NOTHING NATURAL about Central Park. Here the original mother is a stepmother.

Welcome, lovers, to Central Park!

In 1848, New York City was deciding whether or not to spend money on the project "Central Park." The mayor of the city, **Fernando Wood**, bravely spoke out for the park, arguing that New York City was destined to be one of the great cities of the world and this park would be one of the essential ingredients of that eventual greatness.

Fernando Wood owned about 30 percent of the property around the perimeter of the proposed park. The mayor profited from the original construction of the park more than any other single individual in the city.

This is how something like Central Park gets built in New York City. And Central Park's survival is an even more bizarre, unexplainable, even metaphysical truth**. The most important statistic about Central Park is that it is STILL HERE.** In a city where avaricious real estate speculation is a religious thing, 842 acres of parkland has persisted.

It was in the mid-1840s that New Yorkers first begin discussing the possibilities of building a large public park down the middle of the island. The original land—from 59th Street to 106th Street—cost five and a half million dollars.

The land, at that time, was occupied by immigrant villages that paid meager rent, living out mercantile lives in small brick and stone huts. The private landowners profited greatly from the sale of these villages to the city in the name of creating this theoretical public park. As you enter Central Park now, take a moment to fully realize that you are entering a bounteous ecosystem that was, not long ago, literally a blueprint. *THE TREES ARE LAUGHING.*

The man predestined to design Central Park was named **A. J. Downing.** He was and still is a major influence in naturalistic landscape architecture. Naturalistic, which is to say, creating an ecosystem of rhapsodic, seemingly disorganized, botanical journeys that is actually, silently, entirely organized.

A. J. Downing dies in a bizarre boating accident off the coast of the Bronx when Central Park is still a zygote.

Calvert Vaux was four feet, seven inches tall. This is really all the biographical information one needs to grasp his architectural style. He was a brilliant young architect from London who had come to New York to apprentice with A. J. Downing.

Frederick Law Olmsted was a renaissance man who had written a book of editorial observations about his trip through the antebellum South. He was also a great traveler and aficionado of parks. Olmsted was hired as the superintendent of Central Park. Superintendent, which is to say, a general in charge of forcibly evicting any immigrants who did not want to vacate their homes. In New York City history, evicting people for the sake of raising the value of a property is called *morality* and sometimes *gentrification.*

The city sponsors a contest and thirty-six architects draw up their plans for what the proposed park should look like. Frederick Law Olmsted lassoes Calvert Vaux, arguing that as superintendent of the land he knows the movements of the land better than anyone. Together, Olmsted and Vaux create **"The Greenswards Plan"** and together they win the contest.

They worked on the park together for eighteen years. No one can be sure which man particularly, specifically, created what. Vaux is often given credit for the architecture and Olmsted for the landscaping. They argued toward the end and even charged each other with plagiarism. All good rock 'n' roll bands begin with half-lives. We know what happened to **Lennon and McCartney.** At the peak of **The Clash**'s popularity, Mick Jones and Joe Strummer were getting into fistfights offstage. **DISSONANCE is a faster way into the soul sometimes than harmony.**

Vaux went on to design major landmarks in New York City. The **Tilden House** on Gramercy Park is one of the great residences in Manhattan. His **Jefferson Market Tower** on 10th Street and Sixth Avenue is fairy-tale architecture commenting on its own purpose: **a courthouse that laughs.**

Olmsted became the major landscape architect of his era. He designed the ramparts around the Capitol building in Washington, D.C.; Mont Royal in Montreal; the arboretum in Boston, and he would co-author the plans for Yosemite park. He invented the idea of the "parkway," a beautiful vision, truly. He understood that there would be enormous roads bestriding the continent, so he pushed forward the idea that they should all be parks in motion so that the transportation of this country would be continually escorted by nature.

As we enter the vast park now, acknowledge formally that you are currently entering your own being.

A WALK FROM THE REFLECTION POOL TO STRAWBERRY FIELDS:

Note the **Reflection Pool** at 59th Street and Fifth Avenue, the receptacle/aftermath of a swamp that once lived out its mooshiness in this place. Here, the two essential architects of Central Park, Frederick Law Olmsted and Calvert Vaux, drain the swamp and build up an artificial hillside creating a sacrosanct, tranquil poolside that is protected from the chaos of 59th

Street, and filled with largemouth bass to entertain the city's compleat anglers.

The plan was—is—quite prophetic since 59th Street was—is—not nearly as chaotic as planned.

The **Reflection Pool** often has **ducks** floating on it. **They are on the payroll,** thespians performing their roles with clear and present objectives and thus contributing to the enormous theatricality called Central Park.

Descend the stone staircase that cascades down to the water and walk along the aquatic edge. The Reflection Pool was once twice the size it is now. Half of the water was drained by the Parks Department in the 1930s. **Robert Moses,** a major player throughout New York City's urban planning during that era, was one of many arguing for a transition in Central Park's public status.

Moses was a man of the twentieth century arguing that this nineteenth-century transcendentalist locale was destined to become a twentieth-century recreational facility. And so, symbolically, under his regime, half of the Reflection Pool is drained and becomes **Wollman Rink** an ice-skating-sometimes-roller-skating rink.

Frederick Law Olmsted, according to legend, saw a group of boys playing a primordial form of baseball on the lower lawns in the 1860s and at that moment outlawed baseball from the park. The transcendentalists who built this park thought of it as a place to scintillate with trees, to sit with grass, and to stare into one another's eyes. **No sweating allowed in the original Central Park**—no perspiration of any kind. Anyone you see here today congregating for soccer games, jogging, or rollerblading—they are not historically accurate. Anyone you see here today sunbathing, lounging, picnicking, contemplating, or kissing—they are historically accurate.

As we move up past the bridge, notice the rooftops of the **Central Park Zoo.** Take a moment for a cartwheel and a deep breath. Breathe in positivity and breathe out negativity, and with that simple action you are in keeping with the true purpose of the park. True purpose, which is to say, you are with this simple action in keeping with your own true purpose.

Some brief glimpses of the Central Park Zoo: A menagerie was started here during the first year of the park's construction. Animals were dedicated from nations around the world to congratulate the park on its birth. In the **Central Park Conservancy Archives** they have Calvert Vaux's drawings of some nests, nests that were destined to be resting underneath geese that were destined to be arriving from Norway. Vaux designed all the water fountains here, the benches, all the streetlamps; this was a compulsive man. I am sure the geese would agree with my analysis.

The zoo is orchestrated by levels. The seal tank is on the ground level. *The polar bears float and experience a unique brand of dysfunction on the second level.* At the top level there is a large rock inhabited by monkeys. Watch carefully as they fidget with quiet wisdom and flirt with each other, **Central Park South** erupting into the sky behind them. This is a theater piece unwinding all day long, every day, on 64th Street.

Walking farther up the large road, which curves a bit to the left, you will see **statues of Columbus and Shakespeare** facing each other. Both men are representatives of the state of being fearless in the realm of experience, and are the formal presenters to the botanical prelude to 840 acres of naturalistic landscape.

This botanical prelude is known as "the mall," a procession of two lines of elm trees, on either side of a long promenade, meeting in midair to create a vaulted, cathedral-like ceiling of green leaves.

Walk down this formal introduction presented to you by the designers of this fantasy, and be sure to greet each elm tree and note how each tree has its own individual alignment of limbs. **Each tree is greeting you with SPECIFIC GESTURES.** On the far left, **Sheeps Meadow** is a glistening, green beach that, depending on the season, may or may not be covered in bikinied women, topless male sun worshippers, and other flesh endeavors that make me think life is worth living. The Sheeps Meadow was originally, in the Greenswards Plan, destined to be a military parade grounds. This might have been fun, but instead it became a meadow with an actual sheep flock complete with a shepherd who was on the city payroll. Twice a day, the shepherd would interrupt the flow of traffic on the **East Drive** and escort the sheep to and from their fold, which was a brilliant Victorian shed designed by an associate of Calvert Vaux's named **Jacob Wrey Mould.** Mould would also eventually design the enormous balustraded staircases of **Bethesda Terrace**—the architectural climax to the lower park.

By the 1930s, the sheep flock along with the whole park was experiencing dishevelment. **The sheep flock in particular was trapped in a GROTESQUERIE of SOAP-OPERA INCIDENTS, UNSPEAKABLE NON-FAMILIAL SODOMY, and INCEST.** The sheep flock's gene pool gurgled with the truth of bad economic planning. They were split up and their presence on their meadow ceased to be. However, the Victorian sheepfold remained.

At this simultaneity, Robert Moses has just destroyed the essential restaurant of Central Park's jazz age named **The Casino.** "The Casino," Robert Moses proclaimed, "is undemocratic and only serving to the elites of society."

Of course, Robert Moses was probably mostly interested in derailing the operations of **Mayor Jimmy Walker**, himself one of the great and corrupt politicians of New York's early twentieth century and the owner of The Casino, and one of Robert

Moses's arch political rivals. Moses decides to replace The Casino with his own more democratic invention named **Tavern on the Green.**

Jacob Wrey Mould's Victorian shed, once a sheepfold, is utilized as the centerpiece to a structure that, taking Mould's themes, creates a cacophony of huts designed to conjoin in a central ballroom. The building is, today, a fabulously original series of outgrowths, and is America's most successful restaurant. **ITS MAIN DINING ROOM WAS/IS A DINING ROOM FOR SHEEP,** however.

It is important to be aware of the symbols. That is the only real reason for history to exist.

Eventually Robert Moses plans a large, concrete driveway to unravel in front of the main entrance of Tavern on the Green, a highly recommended pasture for limousines. Neighbors of the meadow area that rests in front of Tavern on the Green hold hands in front of the bulldozers when they come to molest the property with concrete. The population and community-board members resisted the idea of concrete replacing the meadow they had come to adore. This postponed Moses's activities and after a few weeks of wrestling with a judge, he would pounce on the property, with bulldozers, one unsuspecting night under a full moon, and when everyone woke up the next morning there was a parking lot in front of Tavern on the Green.

This would tinge Moses's reputation as a parks commissioner and he would resign soon after. Personally, I find the parking lot beautiful. It is such a crazed correlation to everything else happening around it. Of course, I also long ago equated all concrete in the city with flesh. **Yes, concrete is flesh on this island.** *It pants and sweats and scars and yearns to be stroked.* As we walk the streets, we are eroticizing them. And so, understandably, from my own point of view, the parking lot is rather erotic.

Back on the mall we approach a clearing. This is the **bandshell** and its accompanying benches. The benches recently built by the Central Park Conservancy are based on an original Calvert Vaux design.

The Central Park Conservancy is a nonprofit consortium of New York individuals who formed in the early 1980s when this Central Park was experiencing, and really feeling, the recession. In 1982, the Parks Department had assigned two gardeners to handle the responsibilities and the digging that goes along with 842 acres. The park's upkeep would always undulate along with the American economy and there have been several nonprofit organizations of New Yorkers in the park's history supporting its preservation in transactionally challenged times.

The bandshell was a point of recent contention as it had been donated by a private family in 1903, and that same family had just offered money to renovate it. Public outdoor **concerts** have happened in Central Park from the very first day. They used to put string quartets on rafts and send them out to the center of the **Boat Pond.** ***Stand for a moment in the echo of that aquatic anecdote, and listen to the passion of the violins.***

The Central Park Conservancy, now handling about 50 percent of the park's administrative duties along with the Parks Department, rejected the family's offer to refurbish the bandshell. The conservancy replied that its plan was to remove the bandshell entirely and send it to Peekskill. There was a popular outrage. "Who is this Central Park Conservancy to tell us what public facilities we are going to have or not have in our supposedly public park?" cried members of the populus.

Take a moment away from this melee of human activity and tree branches to consider the matter for a momentary moment, have yourself a democratic philosophical interlude, and during said interlude ask yourself an essential question, a question that has caused the greatest anxiety in Central Park's ongoing existence (a question that has caused even more anxiety than all the failed botanical experiments, *a question you can still hear cried out by the poltergeist energy of the long-dead strawberry plants*—twenty-five hundred of them—that died mortified and insignificant deaths in the artificial soil of **Strawberry Fields**): What is a public park, anyway?

All the parks of New York City began as private institutions. A park, according to the European definition, has a gate around it, with a lock, and the owners to the keys to that lock are the aristocracy living around the immediate perimeters of it. Central Park is the first truly public park in New York history. There are some historians who will insist that the promenade at Battery Park was the first public park in New York City. **HISTORICAL ACCURACY IS NO FUN.**

We know that human history wouldn't be the human history it has been if having fun were at the forefront of everyone's mind. **Fun** is so often overlooked. It is the most vital lesson the human race must learn if it is going to survive on this planet.

For our purposes, Central Park is the first public park in New York City. On the first day of Central Park's opening, there are official signs up at the eighteen different entrances to the original park. These signs read OFFICIAL RULES AND REGULATIONS ON HOW TO ACT IN A PUBLIC PARK, NO HORSE CARRIAGE RACING, NO FIRES, AND NO BATHS.

The Boat Pond was/is the original ice-skating rink and it was/is there that different classes of New York culture congregate in a public place with a common goal in mind. It is also the first place, in 1858, where New York women publicly exhibit their ankles, certainly the place where I would have been as a citizen in 1858.

New Yorkers from the very beginning have not known who should actually administrate this strange organism that we call a public park. Every time you stroll past a KEEP OFF THE GRASS sign in Central Park take a moment to ask yourself, "Who says?

Who is making this demand? Who exactly is recommending this censorship of my current options/possibilities for pursuing my fullest amplifications of self on this day in this place?"

It is a debate that will hopefully never be resolved because at its heartbeat is the very question of **democracy.** What is democracy? The answer, I think: impotency justifying itself. At its best, a democracy is a series of ongoing questions that never find answers. Which is to say, **DEMOCRACY is actually an IMPOTENCY justifying itself.** Which is to say, democracy and myself are, ultimately, the same.

Moving farther along now, we cross the **72nd Street transverse** and behold Bethesda Terrace. The boat pond in front of us is a giant bathtub. It has a drain and pipes running below it. When the water gets too high they pump a little water out. When the water gets too low, they pump a little water in. The Bethesda fountain sprinkling sprinkles with truth—manifested. ***Truth is a flowing that flows for the sake of flowing.*** Notice that truth's physical action is taking place with your saliva in the back of your throat right now.

Bethesda is a reference to the biblical story of the angel that touches the waters of Bethesda and gave them healing powers. The **Croton Aqueduct System** was a series of aqueducts and watersheds built during the 1840s that brought water all the way from Croton-on-Hudson to the city. This was an ambitious attempt to bring clean water to the poverty stricken of the city. The Croton water is, in fact, the first clean water the impoverished have access to on a daily basis thus ending abruptly the long chapters of cholera and typhus that ran throughout the city's unfolding history. The first water that ran through Bethesda fountain is from Croton—the modern, literal Bethesda waters of New York City.

Emma Stebbins was/is the sculptor of the statue of the angel on top of the fountain. Note, the angel's graceful hands touching the flowing water. This statue is the only statue in the entire park that was actually commissioned by the city.

The enormous staircases of Bethesda Terrace have four balustrades, each one sculpted with a sculpture representing the four seasons of the year. The whole thing looks like some strange forgotten entrance to Versailles. When you walk down them to the esplanade, suddenly you're in Venice.

Bethesda Terrace: How would Gene Kelly climb this staircase?!

The Venetian arches that are such gorgeous references to San Marco Square are the fantastic marble of a fun-and-games architecture that refuses to take itself seriously.

Somewhere just off the western ramparts of Bethesda Terrace, Olmsted and Pilat—the original gardener of Central Park—planted two **giant sequoia trees.** These are the truly enormous trees that grow in the redwood forests of California. These trees are the largest living organisms on this planet.

The two sequoia trees fail fairly soon after they are placed in the superficial, vivacious, chameleon soil that forms the stage for this theater piece.

The planting of the two great sequoia trees, however, is representative of how improvisational and informal the original designers of this fantasy are. They are not orchestrating a succinct, formal garden. They are wild.

As Justin Ferate once said, ***CENTRAL PARK is the DISNEY WORLD of the NINETEENTH CENTURY.***

Let us then dance and prance our way up the rockbed staircase that will echo the line of the boat pond's amorphous shape. We are ascending **tremendous rocks.**

And the rocks are the original ingredients of this landscape. And all of Manhattan—the metropolis that it is today—is a geology poem written by these rocks. There is only one passable pedestrian roadway connecting Lower Manhattan to Upper Manhattan for the first one hundred and fifty years of this city's supposed existence. Up until the 1830s, it was easier to get uptown by boat than it was by land.

Rock. Note the rock. Did I mention the rock? **The rocks are speaking. They are reminding us that we are in this current space-time continuum actually trapped between two ice ages.**

Rock. Climb the rock. Feel the rock under your feet. That strength you feel, this strong connection to the earth and the complete fortitude building itself from the hardest matter of all. The force of this alert, harsh substance causing your body to stand up straighter than usual, feel that force. This is the force that built New York City.

Note the rock. *The* **rock** *is LAUGHING at all this strange interplay occurring on its backside.* It is as inanimate as we are.

Did I mention the rock? The whole city is formed from it. At the lower point of the island today there are large out croppings of enormous buildings; all of them are outgrowths of the powerful rock that formed there when the Wisconsin glacier melted. We conveniently refer to this as the Financial District.

There are enormous, profound vaults dug into the rock of Lower Manhattan. Chasms imbued with societal purpose. The Federal Reserve Bank is there, for instance. It is the second-largest gold reserve of the United States, second only to Fort Knox. It is protected by ninety-ton steel doors. This is all made possible by the enormity of the rock.

The rocks north of the Financial District sink. This creates a meadow that was known as **Lispenard's Meadows**. What develops there? TriBeCa, Greenwich Village, SoHo, Chelsea . . .

districts that later become famous for preserving their nineteenth-century allure. This preservation was not the work of preservationists or poets. It was the work of the rock. It was where the rock was and is.

The hard, truthful bedrock is so sunken below the topsoil in this area of the island that it is much more expensive, much more difficult to build big buildings there.

The rock erupts abruptly to create Midtown Manhattan. The foundations for the Empire State Building reach fifty feet into the ground. A shallow hole was dug to make way for 102 stories of granite and stainless steel, but the rock is so solid and so near the surface of 34th Street, one need only dig a shallow hole to build a colossus.

The rocks continue throughout Central Park and just think of all the gunpowder and dynamite and perspiration and mules it took, over a period of eighteen years, to remove the rocks from their natural fortifications. The rocks that remain are entertained, on a daily basis, as they bear witness to the most complicated mammal on the planet try to enjoy the afternoon.

The last four blocks of Central Park are virtually donated to the city after the land had been purchased below 106th Street. Landowners there were confident that the rocks were so large they could never be tamed properly for real estate speculation.

The rocks suddenly sink again, creating plains. We call this **Harlem.**

Escalating in the northern reaches of the island, the rocks jettison and form ramparts and treachery that has still not been civilized by the most outrageously avaricious. Those rocks are the archaic punctuation to everything happening to the south of them.

All of Manhattan is an enormous sculpture chiseled from solid, solid rock. An enormous work of art, which is to say, creativity is each of our attempts to get back to the original exuberance we came into this life with. ***Creativity is our faces as the infants that we once were,*** traveling. Traveling across the horizon of our lives. We came into this world thrilled to be here.

I am sure the rocks would agree with my analysis.

Rock. Note the rock. And on the other side of this path we are walking through the rocks and paralleling the shoreline of the Boat Pond. We find ourselves with an astonishing vista view of the expanse of the Boat Pond and the **Central Park West** skyline. An astonishing extemporaneousness totally orchestrated.

Every rivulet and turn of this park is carefully planned out by Victorian men fighting off their own repressed selves. You can feel it in the pathways' purposeful U-turns.

At this point, I would like to look out at this divinely inspired naturalistic design and ask the architect himself—man to man—"Would you be such a lover of nature if you did not have such control over it?"

And **beauty** is an experience. An experience in limitlessness-NESSnesssssNeSsssssssssssssNESSnesssNeSss. The appropriation of beauty, which is not experiencing it, seems to be the essential fad of this current consciousness the human race has, ever more perplexed, stumbled into.

Controlling the beauty in our lives is ourselves controlling the beauty of ourselves. Central Park is, therefore, also a great landmark in the diagramming of self-censorship.

The universe breathes through chaos, and hence, nature is chaotic. **Civilization is a denial of nature. A denial of Nature, especially, as she RUNS CRAZED and ALIVE through our veins. Therefore, Central Park.**

A sample of nature's chaos we can enjoy from the sidelines, almost participate in; this vista view is ourselves as voyeurs and cheerleaders along the sidelines of our own lives. Direct experience is something we reserve for certain special episodes of frothing salivary afternoons. And this vista view is posing for us, displaying itself as an advertisement for nature.

The human race is deeply alienated from its original planetary role. ALIENATION HAS BECOME THE MOST HUMAN OF ALL ATTRIBUTES.

One of the very first mythologies civilized man passed down to this vista view and this moment is the story of **Gilgamesh.** The Sumerian who cuts down the Tree of Life. This is the first activity that appeals to Gilgamesh. This is happening in a place where there were not too many trees.

The human race is deeply alienated from itself. The appreciation of itself. This is the true reason Central Park is built. It is an ongoing, alive attempt to appreciate ourselves. Central Park is nature fenced in. Does that sound familiar to your experience?

Walk down the knoll called **Cherry Lane.** The rounded fountain was originally a horse-carriage turnaround. All the major drives of Central Park are originally gravel paths designed for horse carriages.

"The Falconer" statue on a ridge overlooking the 72nd Street transverse is an example of Central Park statuary that is making more of an attempt to work itself into the romanticism of the landscape, as opposed to, for instance, the large statue of **Daniel Webster** that is staring down the whole place.

Webster's famous speech is encapsulated on the pedestal of the statue. The speech was orated in front of Congress during the heated anecdote called the **Nullification Crisis of 1832.**

President Andrew Jackson had just passed a series of tariff bills that were supportive to the manufacturers of the North and, simultaneously, destructive to the slave owners of the South. Vice President Calhoun recommends that his home state of South Carolina secede from the union, claiming "states' rights."

States' rights, which is to say, an understanding that the United States is a contract signed onto by several sovereign, autonomous states. Any one of these states, therefore, can pull out of the contract. With this argument, South Carolina leaves the Union, and this results in presidential orders that its perimeters be surrounded by the National Guard because of this at times subdued, other times outlandish, contract. We call this the United States.

The Nullification Crisis of 1832 is an anecdote that becomes a foreshadowing of the American Civil War, which begins thirty years later.

Webster is a politician with a great chin. His words are powerful words and they affected several groups of people in 1832, groups of people who really believed in themselves. However, *the original designers who have brought you surreptitiously through hills and dales to this place didn't want you worrying about the* ***Nullification Crisis of 1832.***

That legislative conflict and Webster's dogmatic posture reminds us that we are surrounded by a city. And this leads us back to the reminder that we are citizens of a city. Eventually, Webster reminds us of taxes, meetings, rent, hygiene, and the many other trivialities that place controls over our lives.

Take a moment to compare Webster's vision of *union* and the tree's version behind the statue. If there is anything Mother Nature yearns for, perhaps, it is fresh, new interconnections between living organisms on the planet. If this is so, New York City—a bonanza of original symbiosis—is a great triumph of Mother Nature. In this regard, Central Park is New York City's greatest self-portrait.

The original architects fought off this kind of statuary because they thought any cosmopolitanism referred to in a romantic locale would interrupt the journey. Daniel Webster and many other statues in the park are interruptions. Just as

Central Park is an interruption to the grid plan of this city and is an enormous interruption to the avarice and instant gratification that has always been the preferred method of living and doing business on this island.

There is no way to get from point A to point B in this park unless you can fly. If you come into this park in a rush, you are finished. Your practical agenda and focused destination are eaten alive by pedestrian paths that hook and turn on themselves. This is 842 two acres planted in the middle of enormous practicality; planted in the name of impracticality. This place has no allegiance to linear time or to any of the precise, meticulous political slogans we sell ourselves into other lives with, which is to say, **this is 842 acres of INTERRUPTION paying homage to all INTERRUPTIONS everywhere.**

Central Park is a reminder, at times an alarm sounding off, that insists the most important and incredible events of our lives make no sense.

As we come to the close of this tour, this journey through our own forests resulting in our own clearing, this series of moments giving dictation, this dance between who we are and who we might be, let us walk to the top of this recently rehabilitated green, running hillside and ask the anti-Cruise, also known as the limits we set upon ourselves, this: "What is practical about love? What is sensible about surrender? What logic can you find in compassion?"

Strawberry Fields was a million-dollar botanical rehabilitation initiated by Yoko Ono. She is the widow of John Lennon—the famous Beatle—a being who played music and lived and died musically. Over one hundred apparatuses of botany were dedicated and planted in this place by nations from all over the world, planted and growing in the name of peace.

Stand on the **Imagine** plaque placed in the concrete-flesh ground among the various flora and fauna.

Stand on this word "Imagine" and imagine yourself as healthy and happy; imagine someone you love as healthy and happy; *imagine that this OPULENT TANTRUM we conveniently call the World is an unfolding twenty-four-a-day miracle* and imagine that you are standing in paradise right now.

And then, realize that it is true.

A Tour of the Statue of Liberty: Stay Free

The statue of liberty is a lazy bitch.
—Ice Cube

The Statue of Liberty, a colossus, the American sphinx, is a small landmark compared to the situation it catalyzes.

*

THE STATUE OF LIBERTY (OFFICIALLY ENTITLED "LIBERTY ENLIGHTENING THE WORLD") IS A MINOR LANDMARK COMPARED TO THE SITUATION IT CATALYZES.

*

New York City, the great sculptor-situationist, has crafted an awe-inspiring assemblage slung across three islands. The basic in short, all the ingredients of ourselves and our attempt to cop our inalienable rights—life, liberty, and the pursuit of happiness.

Here, the city is teaching us that **freedom** is the ability to feel bliss in a long line.

FREEDOM *is finding*
BLISS in LONG LINES.

When you can celebrate and be psyched to be alive while standing in the middle of a long line, you're free. Your problems have become play dates, your behavior is a playmate, and your detours are treasure maps leading to the elusive dream for which the statue is dedicated. **(For more about freedom, refer to the greatest moments of your life.)**

Other ingredients of this *Statue of Liberty situation* are a harbor, three parks (Battery, Liberty, and Ellis), a large statue personifying liberty, an immigrant station that is now an immigrant museum, a fleet of motorized boats called ferries, two intact fortresses built to protect the harbor in 1812, and many lines of people that vary greatly in length and purpose.

The situation is lived out and in constant motion from early every morning until dusk.

Its precise hours of operation vary from season to season.

One enters this Sisyphus contest by entering **Castle Clinton,** the great rounded fortress that stands on the outer lip of **Battery Park.** Castle Clinton has never fired a bullet even though it has been equipped to do so since 1812. In its spotlit moment, Castle Clinton went ignored by the British who chose, instead, to invade Baltimore. This way **Francis Scott Key** could be kidnapped at Fort McHenry and write the **Star-Spangled Banner** as a prisoner of war aboard a British vessel. Castle Clinton never got to be part of any of that. It sat in the shadows of all action, a fortress awaiting its true purpose.

By the mid-nineteenth century, Castle Clinton was known as Castle Garden. It had become the original immigrant station of New York City before Ellis Island was initiated for that purpose. In Yiddish the word *kesselgarden*, based on the words *Castle Garden*, means *chaotic place.* At that time, **THIS IMPOTENT FORTRESS STOOD IN AN ONGOING, GRACEFUL SURRENDER AS IT WAS OVERRUN BY A BEDLAM OF REFUGEES, ABANDONED CHILDREN, AND EXILED RADICALS.**

At the turn of the century, Castle Garden, still coming down from the high of being an immigrant station, evolved into a grand theater that housed many famous performers and performances of the time.

Today, Castle Clinton, no longer a theater itself, serves as the box office for a much larger theater piece. It is within this armed fortress that one purchases the tickets that lead to the boat ride that leads to Lady Liberty.

Park rangers and other officials stand around formal signs and ropes where the **ticket line** forms. All the accoutrements around the ticket line breathe with ***the authority of opportunistic necessity.*** Nowhere is there a sign telling us that **Liberty Park**, the island where the statue stands, is a national park and is therefore free. The ticket gets you admission to the boat ride, not the park.

Once the ticket is purchased, the visitor to the statue exits the side of Castle Clinton facing the harbor. There, awaiting the visitor, is a windswept promenade filled with street vendors selling hot dogs, T-shirts, cotton candy, and assorted tchotchkes. Street performers, often acrobats from the West Indies, a woman painted and dressed up as Lady Liberty (available for photographs), and a wide variety of concerts performed by musicians as varied as a lone trumpeter playing jazz standards to a Chilean band playing songs usually sung to serenade the Andes Mountains.

We have just entered the world of the boats and the operation that operates it.

Here we go to the end of the enormous line (in the summer months the line promises, on average, **sixty to ninety minutes of waiting**), and echo the latest shoreline of Manhattan Island. Most of the time, the line is completely still as it waits for the next ferry to pull in. The ferry boats ride out from the Battery Park docks and sail directly to Liberty Island. They unload themselves, and then are loaded with the enormous line waiting for them on Liberty Island's dock (this line is on average, in the peak of season, a **forty-five minute wait**). The ferries then sail from Liberty Island to Ellis Island. There they unload and load again, the line waiting for them at the Ellis Island dock is also quite long (**forty-five minutes**), and then the people being taken from Ellis Island are ferried to Battery Park and unloaded to exit, the situation having completed the circuit.

Another inevitable addition to the situation has been **corruption.** In civilization, **creation** and **corruption** are **synonyms**.

The boat operation that transports the millions of souls who sail out to the statue each year is a system of profiteers profiting just as profiteers have been doing on this harbor for the last four hundred years. **They are making money transporting people to a free park.**

One might think it would be a group of people humbled by the responsibility of taking people out to the mascot of all they struggle for; no, if you ask them they will tell you they are *just doing their job.*

Just doing their job is the idiom Americans go to when they are **justifying mediocrity**, **apathy**, and ***corruption***. **Professionalism** is the language two Americans go to when they are telepathically admitting to each other that they do not know each other at all.

A seemingly important part of these boatmens' jobs includes

the practice of walking up and down the long line, making sure everyone in it has a ticket. No one is allowed to economize the amount of waiting by seperating from their group and standing in the ticket line where tickets are purchased while, in that simultaneity, the group wades through the first third of the enormous line leading to the actual boat ride. If people are caught by the boatmen in line for the boat ride without a ticket, the boatmen roughly order them back to the end of the line. For many, to be exiled to the back of a ninety-minute line after standing in it for thirty minutes is the worst hell imaginable.

The boatmen's exile of these unfortunate souls caught in the line for the boat ride without a ticket often results in loud retorts stated in their native tongues. All along the line, you can witness the spontaneous combustion of rage and despair erupting in languages from all over the world.

Inevitably, the boatmen have another solution to this sudden dilemma. I have seen this conversation spoken silently between so many, and yet it still blows the mind, **how fluent everyone is in the LANGUAGE of CORRUPTION**. For a quick bribe of usually between twenty dollars and forty dollars, the exiles are allowed to keep their place in line.

Incredible, that so many endure all this just to get to the gift shop.

I have been through this circuit of corruption a hundred times. Only one time have I been to the Statue of Liberty and actually found it liberating.

On this particular summer day, I was assigned the all-day tour for Gray Line. I stood with a group of hollering adults for an hour and a half in line just to get on the boat that sails out to the Statue of Liberty. The boat itself was filled to capacity and we were all squashed insignificantly against the walls as I tried to explain to my group of *seventy*, one at a time, that due to our schedule and the long lines, they only had thirty minutes with the actual statue before they had to get back into another hour-long line to go to Ellis Island for yet another series of lines.

An American woman with two children, who were melting before my eyes in the ninety-degree air, screamed at me, "What kind of tour is this?! We've flown all this way to see the Statue of Liberty and you're giving us thirty minutes with her?! All we do is stand in lines?! Is this what I *paid* for?!"

The Statue of Liberty began as a discussion between French intellectuals in several cafés around Paris about preserving democracy in France. The sculptor, **Bartholdi**, on a boat ride from France to New York City saw the perfect island where the statue could stand prominently in the middle of New York's harbor—the gateway to the New World.

POETICALLY, THE ISLAND HE WOULD INHABIT WITH COLOSSAL FREEDOM WAS A PRISON. **Bedloe's Island** was a work camp, complete with a gallows, before it became **Liberty Island.**

Bedloe's Island sits next door to Ellis Island, which was only then just beginning its new life as an immigration station. Bartholdi's choice of placement for the Statue of Liberty was aesthetic. He knew it would be a shocking event, emanating from the water at the end of a transatlantic journey to New York, but he had no idea the ramifications this statement would have on the lives of millions of immigrants. The statue is simultaneously one man's self-expression and a symbol for the world. This is because *THE WORLD'S LIBERATION MUST START WITH US.*

Today, the **Ellis Island Museum**, just like the original Ellis Island, is a place where many bring their emotions and are met by cold statistics and crowd control. The museum is a brave opportunity to walk into a living picture-postcard sent to us from the past. There was a time when Ellis Island was one of the messiest places of all time, and now it is presented to us shiny, temperature controlled, and without crumbs. **What happened to all the STAINS?** Don't ask. (**For more about the trend embodied by the renovation of Ellis Island, refer to "Wall Street: The Story of What Happened to Our Intimacy."**)

The Ellis Island officials were famous for amputating and changing immigrants' last names if they found them to be unpronounceable or too long. Imagine the country America could have been if these officials had, instead, added on to unpronounceable names and extended the names that were too long with exaggerated, fun suffixes.

For those who have their own boats, I recommend that you sail to the New Jersey side of Ellis Island. The buildings on that side are elongated brick asylums where the sick and dying and insane were stored. The windows on these buildings are broken, shattered, or just nonexistent. This is an opportunity to see what Ellis Island was like before the renovations.

My cousin Bruce told me he used to go out to Ellis Island in the days when it was a plantation of piles of rubble with antique, manual typewriters tossed on top of them. He saw it fresh when it still reaked of sweat and torment. He said, "It was beautiful." (**For more about Cousin Bruce, refer to "A Tour of Washington Square Park and My Heart: Fear Is Joy Paralyzed," and also refer to the dissolution of our fears.**)

Eiffel, who would become the architect of the **Eiffel Tower**, was the author of the statue's ingenious armature. Built with the same materials and using the same methods that would be implemented in the construction of early skyscrapers, Eiffel's skeleton for the statue is an interlacing frame of iron and steel. Three hundred copper plates form her skin. This outer skin is durable because it operates as an epidermis, which is to say it tightens up in cold weather and expands in heat. ***The Statue of Liberty breathes.***

Bartholdi referred to the statue as "my American."

The famous arm of the statue, with torch in hand, was sent

from the French to the Philidelphia Centennial Exposition and then on to Madison Square Park as an attempt to lure American investors to pay for her foundation and assemblage. Lady Liberty's severed arm drew attention but not money. **THE AMERICANS, AT THAT TIME, KNEW SOMEHOW THAT AN ENORMOUS PERSONIFICATION OF LIBERTY WAS NOT A GOOD INVESTMENT.**

The immense German émigré who had landed in New York from St. Louis to purchase the newspaper called *The New York World*, **Joseph Pulitzer**, freaked out. At this stage in his career, Pulitzer had purchased a barge that he had pushed out to the middle of the New York Harbor every night by tug boats. There, while ebbing and flowing with the waves, he would work, have dinner, and sleep in the middle of the harbor. He insisted that he had become so sensitive to the noise of the city, he could no longer sleep on the land.

The truth of the matter is that **Joseph Pulitzer wanted to become *amphibious*.**

Floating in the middle of the harbor each night, Pulitzer must have had an especial compassion regarding Lady Liberty's placement there. Maybe Pulitzer, as an émigré, was especially hip to the statue's significance. He started a campaign with his newspaper to raise money for the statue's pedestal. He argued vehemently that the statue, as a gift from the French people to the American people, should be built with the money of the people and not with the dollars of a few rich businessmen.

He recommended penny donations, recognizing that the statue's power was in its symbolism and donating even a cent was a symbolic gesture as much as a definite step forward. He printed the names of all those who made contributions, no matter how big or small the donation.

Any great American can recognize the importance of spending money on something impractical. Any great American also recognizes that asking people to do so out loud is a great way to sell newspapers. Therefore, Joseph Pulitzer was a great American.

Richard Morris Hunt, the famous American architect who had designed many notable landmarks, including the Metropolitan Museum of Art (whose façade bears similiarities to the Statue of Liberty's pedestal), was commissioned to design the pedestal. It would be a pedestal supporting a 225 ton woman, standing on the broken shackles of tyranny. The pedestal itself sits on the second fortress from 1812 that is still defending the harbor in its own way.

In May 1885, the French ship *Isere* set sail from Rouen with the Statue of Liberty packed in 220 crates. By October 1886, he was assembled on Bedloe's Island and President **Grover Cleveland**, along with many international emissaries, a twenty-one gun salute, and three hundred ships, officially welcomed her to the New World.

Freudian psychology, which was developing at the same time in the mind of that lover of the world in Vienna, would attest to the fact that President Cleveland and the international emissaries and the twenty-one gun salute that accompanied the greeting of Lady Liberty was actually a celebration of Bartholdi's choice to meld his mother's body and his mistress's face for all eternity.

The statue's most magnificent statement is that liberty happens when we find harmony with all the women in our lives.

"Freedom can be seen in the way we carry our bodies," I thought to myself as I compared the American woman's posture to Lady Liberty. This woman and her two children missed the best frontal view of Lady Liberty in the circular cycle of this situation as she accused me of *ripping her off.*

Turns out, someone had been killed on Madison Avenue and that caused the traffic jam that had made us late getting down to the statue. Since we still had to get all the way back uptown by six o' clock, I had to be callous about the time alotted for visitations with the statue, but that doesn't mean I didn't feel her disappointment.

"Look at yourself!" I fired back at her. "You're hot, you're exhausted, you're confused! You don't know where you are, or where you're going! **You're being told where to go by people you don't trust!**"

Another great view of the statue's profile, the New York City skyline just beyond that Latin nose, came into view and the complaining American woman, so caught up with our drama, missed it as well.

On the way back, the huge conglomeration of international complainers jostling for position used to form in the face of the **World Trade Center** just to the north of Battery Park and rising from the skyline—the ultimate symbol and declaration of transactional independence.

The "Twin Towers" always distrusted each other. They were the tallest buildings in New York City. They were a sculpture entitled, "Sibling Rivalry."

They were twins, each trying to look taller than the other at all times of day and night. Depending on where you stood in the city, one tower always succeeded in looking taller than the other. This is the optical delusion that arises from competitive *behavior.*

Competitiveness is a meek attempt at togetherness, vague intimacy, and it makes sharing impossible; it is one of this population's main addictions. Therefore, the sagacious city made this lesson a priority by making it the most visible aspect of the skyline.

The towers stood back-to-back, the gap between them representing non-communication. The World Trade Towers were the result of a culture that could only speak **the language of competition**. Will the World Trade Towers will ever speak to each other again? The true question between these buildings is answered forever: No, they will not. The buildings so recently disappeared from the Earth are still facts of our existence! The World Trade Towers have dissolved to become one with the greatest enormity of all, the sky.

I continued the conversation with the frustrated woman.

"You were excited about your destination, but now you can sense that you're going to be disappointed by what you find when you get there. It's not what you were expecting it to be."

She was silenced. I had her attention. One of the mystical half-truths about babies is that ***when a baby is crying, if you start crying, sometimes the baby stops crying.***

"This is the closest you will ever be to your relatives—the ones who came through **Ellis Island**, the ones you came to visit today, the ones who wept when they first saw the Statue of Liberty. Now you know why they were weeping. Right now," I proclaimed, "is the closest you will ever get to knowing what it was like to be them.

"The Americans keep killing the buffaloes. They keep finding reasons, one more ridiculous than the next, for killing the original, now lost, sages of America. Why? Because there is something essential that they are missing from the experience and, like spoiled children, outraged, they are taking it out on those who are fully enjoying it.

"Any miracle will tell you that just because you are a miracle does not automatically mean you are miraculous. A miracle, to be miraculous, must have a self-realization, must realize that it is, indeed, miraculous; must be energized by the miracle of itself and must energize everything it touches with miraculousness."

America is a miracle TOO LAZY to be *miraculous*.

Acknowledgments

With everlasting gratitude, I would like to thank the great city-teacher . . . sweet one . . . deathless guru . . . I am your disciple deciphering your message humbly. Thank you for your wisdom, your faith, your vitality, and thank you for all the healing you have guided me through.

Thank you and congratulations goes out to Jill Grinberg and her perseverance. She is a literary angel who has taken on the temporary embodiment of a literary agent.

Thanks to Beau Friedlander, a great co-conspirator, whose publishing career is the greatest Hollywood action thriller I've watched in a long time.

Thanks to Nick Einenkel and Trevor Bundy—comrades in copyediting and big thinking.

This book is actually a cocktail party I've been throwing for an array of tour guides, artists, deities, radicals, gurus, ghosts, happy-go-lucky-frauds, relatives, co-conspirators, philosophers, and botanists.

Thank you to Maimonides, Marcel Duchamp, Jean-Paul Marat, August Strindberg, Richard Linklater, my cousin Bruce Brand, the Mystic Family Circus, Parmahansa Yogananda,

Floridan Gail Oakhem, Desmonde Daisy, Walter Benjamin, Trish in Minneapolis, the man, Isaac Babel, Kev Corrigan and crew, the USF posse headed up by Pedro and Tracy, Gustav Mahler, Gail Firth, Alexander The Great, Jonathan Ari Yudis, all the girls at Sugars, Antonin Artaud, the Chilean Sirens, Paula Hayes, Mem and Dad Levitch, Splice Levine, Tad Low, Piki, Theodor Herzl, Viv Outlaw, Stanley Kops, E.M. Cioran, the Holbrookes, Euripides, Bazooka Jerm Pollet, Kharma Kara, Prometheus, Gertrude Stein, Lao-Tzu, Kathy Dunbar, Mark, Jess, Perry, Esme, David and Frances Levitch, D.A. and Bean, The Specials, Cal, Terence McKenna, Jennifer Carter, Fernando and Lotus Blossom, Federico García Lorca, Valerie Gefner, Salvador Dalí, Ann and Meyer Schiffman, Rockwood Freedom and all his dancing partners, Pan—the God of Joy, Steve—the poet/builder, Aaron James, Ethan Hawke, Rabbi Nachman, Kevin Mandel and his salon, Bruce Ornstein and Ellen Barber, Weezer, Robert Mailer Anderson and all his pals, the Frommer brothers, the Miller brothers, the Lipsky brothers, the Lewis brothers and the Belic brothers, Ed and Deb, Ted But and Bianca, Scott Carlin, Elvis Costello, Ernst Pawel, e. e. cummings, Eliza and Nancy, Topher Jarvis, Spiv out at Groove Farm, Henry Miller, Marty Beller, Yogi Bajhain and all my khundalini yoga instructors, Paul Campbell, Rem Koolhaas, Josh Lucas, Justin Ferate, Draca the Dragon, Charlotta Janssen, Christian Dior, Fred Adler, Goldie and Flansburgh, Rumi, Scott Tallinger, Ralph Waldo Emerson, Franklin, Moses, Scott Beiben and his Philadelphian brethren, Duke Ellington, Monali, Mr. and Mrs. Segal from San Antonio, Clifford Odets, and everyone else who has participated in any of the walking tours over the years.

I'd also like to thank the cynical and the downtrodden for all their inadvertent contributions to my process.

Finally, I'd like to thank all the soldiers of bliss who, trapped deep behind enemy lines, strut.